1/20/69

ANGEL MO' AND HER SON,
ROLAND HAYES

BOOKS BY
MacKINLEY HELM

AFTER PENTECOST
MODERN MEXICAN PAINTERS
ANGEL MO' AND HER SON, ROLAND HAYES

Angel Mo' and her Son, ROLAND HAYES

by

MacKINLEY HELM

ML
420
H25H3

AN ATLANTIC MONTHLY PRESS BOOK

LITTLE, BROWN AND COMPANY · BOSTON

1942

COPYRIGHT 1942, BY LITTLE, BROWN AND COMPANY

ALL RIGHTS RESERVED, INCLUDING THE RIGHT
TO REPRODUCE THIS BOOK OR PORTIONS
THEREOF IN ANY FORM

FIRST EDITION

Published November 1942

ATLANTIC–LITTLE, BROWN BOOKS
ARE PUBLISHED BY
LITTLE, BROWN AND COMPANY
IN ASSOCIATION WITH
THE ATLANTIC MONTHLY PRESS

PRINTED IN THE UNITED STATES OF AMERICA

FOR

ESTHER FISKE HAMMOND

With Love.

Preface

IN THE Epilogue to *Men and Women*, Robert Browning writes to E. B. B. about Rafael's sonnets and Dante's painting. Too full of feeling to be satisfied with expression in a single medium, the painter takes up a pen, the poet fits himself out with easel and brushes.

> Does he paint? he fain would write a poem, —
> Does he write? he fain would paint a picture. . . .

The history of the arts is sprinkled with the names of such amphibia: Michelangelo, Dante Gabriel Rossetti, Leonardo da Vinci, Carlos Mérida; but the name of Roland Hayes is not amongst them.

Roland Hayes, a musician, an artist of song, learned from his Mother Fannie — the Angel Mo' of the book — to keep his eye single. He has never been distracted from the practice of the art of singing by any hankering to become a writer. Specifically, he has resisted the temptation to write his autobiography. If it were meet that the story of his life should be written, as certain people belonging to the world of books designed, then, said the

Preface

musician, let a lot be cast into the circle of his literary friends. A lot was given forth and fell on me, as in old time it fell on Saint Matthias. I do not claim, like the thirteenth Apostle, to have been a witness to every coming in and going out of my protagonist; still, I am a friend of ten years' standing.

On my way to Angel Mo' Farm, in Georgia, I began to think of the prospective biography in terms of a translation from one medium to another. I said to myself, If Roland Hayes can somehow *sing* me the story of his life, I shall try to put it into words. And as a matter of fact, something of the sort very nearly happened. The figurative conception of a translation proved to be not so farfetched as it might have seemed. At least, I like to think that some of the lyrical passages in the actual life have come out with some degree of verbal concordance; although I must confess that like Life, and like early Italian opera, the biography has to march part of the time on the narrower line of the recitative.

There was one point, however, at which I was unable to make my subject's music yield, in translation, to the requirements of traditional biography. I could not make it come out in the third person. I was sitting one summer morning on the veranda of the farmhouse at Angel Mo', gazing across the valley at Horn's Mountain — which was about to become a character in my book,

Preface

as the heath is a character in *The Return of the Native* — when it came to me as right and good that I should tell the story in the first person. Why not? I was seeing the Flatwoods with my own eyes, I was there with Roland while he was re-creating Pa and Ma.

I shall write this book, I thought, as Roland Hayes would write it if he, a man of music, fain would write out his life himself.

After form and mood were so determined, just one serious disability further projected itself into my conscious mind. Mr. Hayes, like Mother Fannie, is so modest and reticent that I, writing, so to speak, in his name, have had to be content with habitual understatement of my own feeling for the greatness of his spirit and his art.

MacK. H.

Brookline
June 28, 1942

Contents

ANGEL MO' AND HER SON,
ROLAND HAYES

I Bury My Father

WHEN Father William blew his hunting horn the Flatwoods shivered. Hounds moaned and quivered and strained at their leashes. The huntsmen licked their lips, savoring the roast possum they would be eating come next day's dinner. The hard pine on Horn's Mountain rocked in the darkness and quickened the quarry to his danger.

Pa's hunting horns were famous in the Flatwoods, the Negro settlement in the north Georgian country-side where I was born. In those days farmers allowed the longhorned cattle to wear the curved horns that Nature gave them, and it was from those bony cores that Pa made horns for the hunt. He shaved them paper thin, clear through the sheath, with splitting knives and small, well-tempered planes. He polished their pearly, opalescent surfaces until they were as smooth and shiny as oak leaves.

With hunting in prospect, perhaps on the night of the new moon after the corn gathering, Pa would take one of his horns down from its peg on the kitchen wall, along about ten o'clock of the evening, and shuffle out into the barnyard to call up the neighboring farmers. He had prodigious lung power. When he called hogs down from the Mountain in the autumn he could be heard all the way to Little Row, the white village three miles up the road; and when he clasped his horn, puffed out his bronzed cheeks, pursed his lips, and strained his breath through the mouthpiece, he produced — you can get out of a cow horn only as much as you blow into it — loud, windy blasts of protracted and full-bodied tone, melodious and powerful and eerie. This was my first remembered music, my introduction to the quality of sound.

My father's colored cronies soon came streaming into the barnyard, some of them afoot, some of them on their ancient nags, all of them with lanterns and torches and tumbling hounds. For a quarter of an hour Pa would din the Mountain with change of key and agitated tremolo, until, with mounting excitement, he had prepared hounds and hunters alike for brave approach to the fearful adventures of the night.

When at last Pa rode out into the darkness towards the pine-covered Mountain, he was his own man. Pa was part Indian, a good part Indian, according to his own account of himself, and he never cared very much for life on the farm. He loved the wild freedom of wood and stream. He used to tell us that he admired the Indian way of bringing up children. Because I was a particularly shy and timid child, he threatened to pitch me into the middle of the muddy Oostanaula, to make a man of me. That, he said, is what his Indian father would have done.

He was something of a man of mystery to his children, my father, William Hayes, of God knows exactly where and whence. When my mother met him on the road from Atlanta to Chattanooga, just after the Surrender, he was carrying in his pocket a document which showed him to be a free man and entitled to passage through the country. He had a notion that he might have been born in Illinois, but it was from Missouri that he went South, in the days of the reconstruction of Atlanta, to find work. What a wonderful carpenter and craftsman my father was! He owned, during my childhood in the Flatwoods, a fine set of matched and graded tools, which he kept neatly laid out and shining like silver in a nearly immovable hickory chest. He could work magic with those tools.

When Pa came across my mother at an encampment of liberated slaves on the highroad running north from Atlanta, he had called himself a doctor. Ma was on her way to Chattanooga with Grandmaw Mandy. She had meant to celebrate the Surrender, news of which had seeped but slowly into those upper counties, by learning how to read and write; and I suppose she took a fancy to my father because he seemed to have the kind of schooling she was determined to get for herself. As for Pa, he lost no time in paying court to the slight and pretty girl who was to be my mother. He married her straightway at the encampment and carried her off to Tennessee.

I have heard from Mother Fannie how Pa, when they lived in Chattanooga, used to come home at night with his pockets stuffed full of scraps of paper, from which he then affected to recite the morbid details of ailments he had treated during the day. My mother was more literal-minded than my father, whose imagination she shortly found to be unmortgaged to strict truth. Unable to believe in one of his uncommonly incredible stories, in which the cure was no less than a miracle, she snatched up a tattered fragment, on a memorable evening, and saw that it was covered with cabalistic scratchings. Although her own learning was deficient, she could see that the penciled marks wanted both rhyme and reason. She thereupon obliged my father to confess that he not only was no physician, but could neither read nor write.

Pa claimed to be of Cherokee stock, and often boasted that he could, at any rate, read and write his own language. We children, in our time, lacked the means to test Pa's mastery of the Indian tongue, but we loved to hear him speak and sing the guttural syllables which he taught us to associate with Indians. In my mother's ears, however, the forms of speech which he passed off as the language of his fathers sounded suspiciously like pig-Indian, and she warned us that Pa was only fooling. It interested me to learn, years later, that the Cherokee idiom had been first reduced to print, in the Sequoyan syllabary, at New Echota, not ten miles from our Flatwoods home.

Clearly, Father never liked the ten-acre farm where I was born, and whither my mother had brought him after the collapse of his professional career in Chattanooga. Nevertheless, he was a good worker — under compulsion. When he had to, he could straddle row upon row of young cotton plants, between daylight and dark, and chop the soil with his hoe in a frenzy of sustained, if impatient, performance. After a day of such passionate labor he felt, I suppose, the need of a durable rest, and the next morning he would find himself a comfortable place in the shade.

Pa taught us children to plow behind an ox named Ned, who wore a bell of a size and bigness of tone which our small farm never quite seemed to require for purely locative reasons. I early suspected my mother of having fixed that bell to Ned's collar so that she might be assured of the continuity of his employment, as well as complacent in the knowledge of his whereabouts.

One hot midsummer day, when Pa had been put to work with the ox in the cornfield, it became evident to all ears that Ned's bell was sounding out an unusual rhythm. Ma, who ever kept both ear and eye upon the problems of our straitened domestic economy, sharply reminded Pa, across the width of field, of the absolute indispensability of his patriarchal occupation. Presently the bell jingled again with obedient regularity. Ma, thinking to reward Pa with a mollifying dipper of cool water from the spring, went out to him in the dust and heat of the afternoon. She found him taking his ease under a shady tree. There he sat, smoking his companionable pipe, and contriving, with a rhythmical motion of his wrist, to produce from a tethered cowbell an audibly convincing imitation of Ned engaged in lawful work.

Years later, in 1926, when I visited Joseph Mann, who had inherited my mother from his father not long before the Liberation, I was reminded of that occasion.

"Roland," said Mr. Mann, "are you that boy of Pony's that got caught settin' down on a plow and ringin' a cowbell?" The story had been told all over the Flatwoods, but it was really Pa, and not I, that got caught.

The forests, not the fields, furnished my father with his substantial contribution to our daily bread. If he liked better to eat than to feed my mother's chickens, he was the man to keep the crafty red fox from the coop. If he had no head for figuring and accounts, he could guess within a few ounces the weight of a treed possum, by noting the size of the tree the hounds bayed under: the smaller the tree, the bigger the possum; and he would know at once whether to shake him or beat him down. At break of many a day in the fall of the year he would appear from the hunt with meat to eat and skins to be traded for salt and flour from the outside world.

If Pa, moreover, was indifferent to the care of barnyard animals, whose domestic habits afford any naturalist only the most intolerable boredom, he knew how to look after his dogs in the neighborhood of a skunk. One whiff of spray and your hound is spoiled for the whole night's hunting. You must pot your skunk, the pretty creature, quickly with your gun, and not let him foul the dogs you are shooting with.

What with the meat Pa fetched from the hills, to supplement Ma's careful husbandry of the produce of the farm, I do not remember that we children — I had six brothers and sisters — ever went hungry. A few steps from the kitchen door stood a smokehouse, with a pit for curing hams and flitches of bacon and sausages. We stuck our hogs just before Christmas, and through the long month of January we tended a hickory fire whose smoke filled the aromatic chamber where the meat was hung, done up in muslin and wired to the rafters. I cannot remember a season, while my father lived, when there was not a piece of smoked meat to flavor our food — the string beans and fresh corn that we ate in the summer, the rice and potatoes of our scantier winter diet.

A small spring bubbled up from the earthen floor of the smokehouse, providing cold storage for milk and butter and eggs during the hot midsummer weather, when out of doors the fierce sun parched our dusty fields; and in a murky corner a twenty-gallon keg of sorghum mounted a pair of concave wooden horses. On warm mornings the sorghum flowed freely into a cavernous pitcher, whence it was poured over our cornmeal mush at breakfast, but in the winter only a little core of syrup remained liquid inside a shell of sugar, and it seemed to me, when Ma sent me out into the chilly darkness of the early morning, that it took forever, drop by drop, simply to sweeten the bottom of the jug.

I Bury My Father

In my childhood I did not blame my father for his want of application to husbandry because I admired so much his wonderful gift for making music. I believed there was no sound in nature that he could not imitate. His voice brought deer, bear, and partridge within range of his gun. He taught me to identify the songs of birds, urging me to harken to them — himself repeating and answering their melodies, over and over again. I learned to distinguish between "true songs," which the male birds sing when they are establishing their private territorial rights in the spring, and the less highly specialized "recordings," as the songs of lonely females and the wintry choruses of gregarious males are indiscriminately called. At the risk of offending my mother, and sometimes at the cost of being whacked with her whip, I used to stop work in the fields to listen to meadow larks, orchard orioles, and summer tanagers — fancying, in the sympathetic way I learned from my father, that I was a bird addressed by my companions in the trees, and birdlike answering them.

When my father called a deer, he was a buck himself. In transactions with untamed life he made an offering of his whole nature. It is perfectly clear to me now that he opened the way for me to become a musician by showing me how to offer my body, in imitation of him, to receive the music which he taught me to discover in the natural world. I learned from my father how the body follows the imagination. If singing is to be a really imaginative art it must give off, on each occasion, the effect of a fresh creation in which mind and body act together. The body must respond freely and newly to the mind's momentary act of re-creation. Thus a song becomes a personal expression, and not merely an animated transcription of the composer's notes.

I early learned from my father to let my imagination do fluently what many singers have learned to do only through the repetitive use of destructive vocal exercises. I am fifty-five years old now, and yet, because my father taught me that the body follows the mind without stress and strain, I am conscious of no wear and tear on my vocal equipment.

II

In order to share my father's secret life in the woods, to hear the mystical exchange of musical sounds, I had to persuade him that I was a fit attendant upon his boldest escapades. Sometimes at night I was charged with carrying a "lightered" to the scene of a hunt: a flaming torch made from the resinous core of an old pine stump. When the hounds struck a hot scent they often traveled so fast, down through a hollow, up over a rise, the huntsmen after them, that I would be left behind. Lost in the darkness of shadows blacker and more terrifying because I was rimmed in the light of the torch I bore, I would outdo the yelping dogs with my howling.

After the hunt I had frequently to carry the victim over my shoulder, and when the angry captive, suspended by his naked, prehensile tail from a split poplar sapling, gave over his natural habit of playing possum long enough to snap at my legs, I was too frightened to hang on to my burden. Old Kirby used to take pity on me and try to teach me to be brave.

"We're all hunters here," he would say. "Hunters ain't skeered, hunters can carry their catch safe home all right."

In the late summer a nocturnal hunt usually came to an end in a watermelon patch. Along about two o'clock in the morning the men would build a bright fire — say on the edge of the big Kemp meadow. They would search the vines for ripe, frosty melons — an experienced thumb and middle finger can detect the sound of honeyed sweetness in the dark — and then, having called all hands and all hounds, they would sit down to gorge themselves until they fell asleep. At daybreak my father would carry me, the carrier, home, still full as a tick of watermelon flesh.

In the winter we used to go bird threshing, a milder sport which didn't so much frighten me. We carried pine torches up and down the fields at night, blinding the birds, the robins and the swallows, refugees from the Northern winter, and when they flew up from the dry grass we struck them down with brooms and barbecued them. What a lovely morsel each bird became, racked over the slow fire of hickory embers!

We went rabbit hunting in the winter, too. Just before my father died he gave me my first small shotgun and let me go rabbiting with Mount, my dog. Suddenly in a snowy field we jumped a cottontail. I forgot to shoot, forgot I had a gun. I dropped my fowling piece and took out after my dog. Together we outran the rabbit and I caught him in the way I knew best, with my fists. Poor Mount came down with rabies, not long after. My brother Robert agreed to shoot him for me, but the shotgun failed to fire. Mount died in agony while the disorder ran its fatal course. We gave him such a funeral as we judged becoming to a nearly human dog. Robert mourned and I preached the funeral sermon.

There are said to be twenty kinds of native trees in

our old hunting country, including eight varieties of oak, and I am confident Pa knew them all. Certainly he knew the shape of every piece of timber growing on Horn's Mountain, and estimated accurately the best uses each could be put to. He made splits for chair bottoms from the smooth-grained white oak; sound beds and comfortable rocking chairs of maple; straight-backed seats and sturdy benches of impervious hickory. He had built and furnished with his own hands the cabin I was born in some twenty years after the War Between the States.

It was only a log cabin of two rooms that he had built, at the foot of Horn's Mountain, near the town of Curryville (it was called Little Row in my childhood); but it had certain marks of distinction in comparison with even ruder houses in the neighborhood. There were two chimneys made of stone pulled out of the Mountain, and the timbers of which the walls were built were stopped not with red clay, according to the local fashion, but with yellow, after my father's whim. He had discovered a small mound of it in a near-by field.

The fireside in the front room was the center of our family life. Opposite the chimney, in the other end of the room, Pa and Ma and Jesse, my youngest brother, slept together in a big maple bed. Jesse, my mother's baby, became a gypsy, and then a sailor, and heard the first bomb explode over London in the first World War; but he was always "Baby" to Ma, even after he ran away.

Pa's rifle, which hung over the bed, caught the firelight at night and brought the far, dark wall to life. I remember how the bursting lights used to glance upon a circle of Victorian picture frames which encased some family photographs. They were gifts, no doubt, of white people my mother worked for when Pa was doctoring in Chattanooga. They were, of course, absurdly inappropriate, but they introduced a note of elegance of which we children were inordinately proud, and they probably explain my choice of Victorian decoration for the farmhouse I live in when I visit my farm in Georgia.

In the small back room of the cabin the rest of us — William, Jr., Mattie, Nathaniel (Tench), John, Robert (called Brantie), and I — slept in little poplar beds turned out on Father's lathe. On the west side of the house, away from the Mountain, Pa put up a weatherboard lean-to in which Ma did the cooking.

I am sure that my mother appreciated Pa's skillful carpentry and his genius as a cabinetmaker, and that she was grateful for all the food he made the forest yield. But it was a mortification to her that he was not also a good farmer and a man of God. The truth is that Pa, although he became a member of the Baptist Church, cared no more for churchgoing than he did for farming. It was probably because Ma was a pillar of the church — a founding member, in fact, of the colored meetinghouse in our community — that Pa was never excommunicated. My Uncle Bill Mann was read out of the society of believers, by reason of habitual non-attendance at worship, and Uncle Bill most generally non-attended church with my father.

We lived behind a clump of cedar trees on a lane leading from the Flatwoods to Mount Zion Baptist Church, where services were conducted by a visiting preacher on the first and third Sundays of the month. Deacons and deaconesses of the Amen corner conducted midweek prayer meetings, and wandering evangelists intermittently appeared to stir up the local religion. My mother always sat in a forward pew on the right-hand side of the church, in the place appointed for women, and took a leading part in the chorus which inspired the preacher with cries of "Amen!" and "Tell us about it, tell us about Jesus." Pa only rarely sat in the section of the church appointed for men. He was usually to be found at home, on a Sunday morning, enjoying his private sabbatical routine.

Until my brother Robert came home from nine-o'clock Sunday school, Pa puttered about the cabin at aimless odds and ends. At ten o'clock his familiar Sunday observance began. Under the hickory tree, where on weekdays he rived white-oak saplings and wove splits into baskets for the cotton pickers — or in front of a roaring fire on a wintry Sabbath — he sat to the tonsorial ministrations of my brother, whose weekly duty it was to plait Pa's long, straight hair. This ritual inevitably recalled to Pa's mind the days when he had lived the tribal life of the Cherokees, and fiercely entertaining were his recollections (or were they fictions?) of that time. When, as it frequently happened, Uncle Bill dropped by to visit my father on the way to church, more often than not he sent my Aunt Maria to hear the Gospel story in Ma's company, while he stopped on to listen to Pa's accounts of less supernatural wonders.

If the visiting preacher intoned theological mysteries that passed my comprehension, I was likely to sit unquietly in church, thinking of my fortunate brother at home. I could picture him smacking his chops over an illicit collation which Pa had prepared when the hair plaiting was done. Perhaps Pa had already acquainted my mother with the disappearance of a young fryer from the chicken coop. Perhaps he had seen a red fox in the cornfield. At any rate, when Ma and I returned from our pious exercises there was never any physical sign or remnant of the bird: feathers burned, bones buried, skillet glistening. Only a look of seraphic satisfaction on three black faces harbored a trace of the secret sin.

On winter nights Father told his stories in front of the fire for the benefit of the whole family. He was a great raconteur; he could make us laugh or cry and cause our crinkly hair to stand on end. One night he came in from the lane, pallid under his bronze skin, and told us that a headless man had followed him all the way home from the neighborhood of Mount Zion Church.

"I done shot at dat critter," he said, "and what do you think he done? He blowed up, big as a house, and jumped right up into de sky!"

Mother did not approve of the fanciful turn Pa's storytelling took, although she sometimes laughed in spite of herself. She used to say that he ought to be teaching his children good wholesome truths instead of alternately entertaining and scaring us. There were times when she quite spoiled our pleasure in Pa's stories, but it never occurred to us to question her judgment. We realized, all of us, at an early age, that Mother and Father were simply different people. I loved them both.

Perhaps once a year Pa would begin to talk about buried treasure, of which there was supposed to be plenty in the Cherokee country. He would tell us that the Big Chief was coming back pretty soon, to look for gold.

"When he comes," he said, "he will go to dat cone of rocks yonder on de Mountain. When he sees dat cut on de wes' side of ol' white oak, he will know where de gold is buried. He will dig it all up, all right."

And then we knew that in a day or two Pa would disappear. Sometimes he would be gone for weeks. When he came back, he would bring us presents; but we never knew where he went.

My brother Robert, who was born with something of the look of the Indian in his face, still hunts treasure in our hills, still has a nostalgic feeling for Indian life. He was fond of our father, and always particularly close to him. I could do the relatively simple work of weaving baskets only with the greatest difficulty and awkwardness, but Robert, who was apt alike with tools and guns, learned to make a wagon as expertly as my father.

I remember that my brothers were not all equally happy at home. Willie, Pa's namesake, ran away after he finished the seventh grade, the highest class in the colored school. News came to us somehow that he had fallen sick down in Alabama, and Pa went to fetch him home. Willie came back crippled, unable to walk without crutches. He had got a cracked knee in an iron smelter. I was always a little in awe of Willie, who had gone to Howard High School in Chattanooga — that was before he went to work in Alabama — and had a better education than some of our teachers in the Flatwoods.

Pa and Willie sometimes had sharp words between them. They really never did learn how to get along together, although Pa taught him how to become the best chair bottomer in the countryside. Ma used to say that Willie had a temper like his Grandpaw Peter, whose father was an African chieftain. One day Father threatened to whip Willie, for some piece of impertinence, and my brother, who went limping about with the help of a crooked stick, cried out, "Pa, you take one step in this here direction and I'll lay you out with this club." Pa let Willie off that time, but it wasn't long before they quarreled again.

I used to feel sorry for Willie. I was mindful of the existence of a cruel and inescapable antagonism between him and my father. Yet Willie was sick; he could never leave home again on his own two legs. It was not long before he fretted himself to death.

Pa was not so severe in judging us, generally, as Ma was, but sometimes he had an abrupt way with him that offended my brothers, as they grew older. He would say, "You don't know no more about dat dan a hawg knows about a side pocket," or, "You ain't got sense to carry guts to a barrel."

Tench and John left home when they were seventeen or eighteen years old. Tench came home sick a couple of times, once for a little while, once for longer. He seemed to be trying to get along with Pa, but by now Ma was beginning to take a strong hand in his affairs. As soon as Tench felt all right he wanted to go out nights, to breakdown dances with the tough crowd that kept away from church. Ma, who couldn't bear late hours and rough company, used to remind him constantly and persistently of his Christian duties. She had an unintermittent way of pounding in the Bible truths, as a good carpenter hammers a nail until the head has disappeared. Tench would soon be off again, to what destination we never knew; until finally, before I was ten years old, he came home to die.

Mattie, my only sister, was a lovable creature, soft and quiet like my wife, our cousin. She was tall and Indian-colored and had a beautiful alto voice. When I was six years old, she married a teamster by the name of Will McClure, who could drive twelve yoke of oxen ahead of a big haul of logs. Will took Mattie to live at Buzzards Roost, in the hills near Tunnel Hill, north of Dalton. It was pretty lonesome for Mattie at

Buzzards Roost. Will rarely came home nights, and Mattie was often alone in her cabin in the dark woods.

She came home on a visit, after a couple of years, and persuaded Ma to let me go back with her for two or three months. We rode the caboose of the daily freight to Dalton and from there we walked the countless miles to Mattie's house. My arms ached with a load of paper bags and packages, my bare feet were bruised and cut on the rocky road.

Mattie's cabin stood in a small, forlorn clearing in the creepy woods, and although I loved my sister, I was deathly homesick there. A curious bird came in the night and pecked at the door of the cabin — a black bird, Mattie said. She thought it was a bad omen, and I felt what Mattie felt, wretched and solitary. The bird was probably digging worms out of the timbers of the cabin, but we only knew that we were out in the high, far hills, with deep forest all around. Sometimes our situation became so insupportable we could not bear it, and then we left in the middle of the night to go to the cabin of some friends — our fright so great that we were willing to risk the horrid walk through the darkness. Pretty soon Mattie took me home again, and before long, entirely abandoned by her husband, she returned to live under my father's roof and fade away and die.

The hand of Death is never very far removed from the

latchstrings of the poor. Only the strong survived the accidents and rigors of our humble Flatwoods life. Still, when sorrow did not press too immediately upon us, we enjoyed our simple sociability. Most of us had too little knowledge of the world to feel that our pleasures were attenuated. Although my mother did not like to have my brothers go to breakdowns, where corn likker and bad girls circulated freely, she was willing to let us enjoy diversions invented by church members. And above all, we learned to make parties of the routine events of our lives.

Sometimes, instead of merely taking a pig to market, we held a barbecue. We have them now, three or four times a summer, on my Georgia farm, and the procedure is not different from what it was when I was a little boy. The big boys and the young men come to the farm in the late afternoon, build a big fire in the barnyard, and boil water in black iron pots. The women and girls stand about arm in arm, rocking on the balls of their feet and talking and giggling; retiring discreetly to a little distance when a pig is stuck, and returning to watch the scalding and the scraping and the dressing.

The pig is racked for the roasting by a pair of oldtime experts, who handle freshly peeled hickory saplings and tying-wires with the beautiful, clean skill of surgeons. Hickory fires are still laid, as they used to be, in shallow pits, and when the red-clay soil is hot beneath the ashes, the embers are raked out. The racked pig is laid over the earthen chamber, and all night long glowing coals from a near-by fire are shoveled into the corners of the pit. In mid-morning, after hours of turning and basting with barbecue sauce, the succulent pork is carved up and handed out, slice by slice, on slabs of homemade bread, to fill a hundred trembling mouths.

III

Occasionally, when I was a boy, I was allowed to watch the dancing at the Garlington house, or at the John Tate farm. Will Garlington had been a notorious infidel, and although public opinion had finally obliged him to join the church, he had never quite been able to put the world away. There regularly repaired to his house all the colored people who wanted to make the most of the church and the world simultaneously, a kind of semi-respectable fringe to the more sedate fabric of our Baptist society. Church people could go to those dances without taking part, but frequently they would be moved to give themselves to dancing and rioting. Then they were likely to be reported to the deacons and brought before the elders, who would exhort them to repent. Unrepentant members were turned out of the church forthwith.

Angel Mo' and Her Son, Roland Hayes

Will Garlington blew the quills at the Garlington dances, and Ren, his brother, one of the neighborhood toughs, cracked the bones and called the sets. The elderly itinerant musician, Jim Kirby, who boarded at our house when he was in the Flatwoods — I called him Uncle Nat — played the fiddle and beat straws, and Jesse Tate picked the banjo.

Many of the musical instruments and a good deal of the music were of African origin. Quills are joints of bamboo, tied together with string in an arrangement like the pipes of Pan. You blow across the open tubes and produce tones like those of a steam piano or calliope, but mellower. In Africa a bone cracker cracks real bones, but in Georgia we used simulacra carved from hickory wood. A good bone cracker can crack bones with both hands, clacking out the rhythms required for buck-and-wing dancing.

The straw beater holds a handful of broomstraws between the second and third fingers of his right hand and brushes them against the strings of a fiddle, in a rhythm which runs counter to that of the fiddler, both fiddler and straw beater performing on the same instrument at the same time. The straw beater has to learn how to keep out of the way of the fiddler's bow, and that is part of the trick of beating straws. I learned to blow quills and my brother Robert beat straws, so that although we were not often allowed to go to the Gar-

lington house, we could make music of our own when
Uncle Nat was stopping with us.

Pete Vaughn, who conducted a seasonal singing
school in the Flatwoods, also used to stay at our house
when he came to the village. He taught me to read
book music, printed in square notes. That was stylish
music, from city hymnbooks. Fortunately, not everybody in our congregation learned to read notes, or our
folk songs might have gone unsung.

There were certain community festivals which the
whole countryside attended, even the church people.
When my mother's brothers, Uncle Wiltsie and Uncle
Simon, picked the banjo — it was Uncle Simon who
invented a name by which I was called in the family circle, Roland-Come-Mumbling-Come-Tumbling-
Come-Paregoric — I was allowed to watch and listen.
Even the church members joined in the clapping of
hands and the singing, although only unbelievers cut
steps and swung their partners.

One of the most popular dance tunes was "Ring
Around, Swing and Play," and it went like this: —

> Ring all around, Suzanne,
> Ring all around, Suzanne,
> Swing all around, Suzanne,
> Swing all around, Suzanne,
> Swing your partners, Suzanne,
> Swing all around.

Angel Mo' and Her Son, Roland Hayes

My mother's cousin, Jesse Tate, of the earringed ears and the sensitive hands — he is still cheerful and engaging at eighty — used to spell my Uncle Wiltsie in calling the sets at "potillias," as cotillions were called in our county. A potillia was formed by eight dancers, four men and four women, who cut the steps in sets of three "bars." A single bar required the execution of various changes: form a circle, hold hands, swing your partners; turn your corners off, turn your partners; promenade, two-and-two, and return your corners; first couple right, second couple left, third couple right, fourth couple left, turn your corners off and promenade. The music and the laughter, the swaying bodies and the shuffling feet, made your own feet itch, if you were a church member and not allowed to dance.

Church people sometimes invited the more respectable musicians to sing and play in the seclusion of their cabins. After an evening of music and storytelling they would serve refreshments of baked sweet potatoes, or perhaps only popcorn and peanuts, hot from the ashes and iron skillets on the hearth. In some houses, never in ours, the older men sat by the fire and told ghost stories over a dram of corn liquor, while the young people pulled syrup candy into brittle threads, white as spun sugar.

So nearly contiguous were the sacred and profane

worlds in the Flatwoods that their music was nearly identical. To be sure, there were different texts, inequalities of mannerism, gesture and vocal expression, and conflicting emotions. Yet, curiously enough, there was very little overt lewdness in the secular songs. Coarseness appeared in them only by implication. There was "The Roustabout Song," for example: —

> Rock me, Julie, rock me,
> Rock me like a baby,
> Rock me slow and easy.

The melody went like a spiritual. With the substitution of the Holy Name for "Julie," you might have had a characteristic religious song. You had to know, you could not have discovered from words or music, that the singer was thinking about a night he had spent with his girl.

It is the greatest misfortune that so little original African music has survived amongst us, the earthy, natural music that our forebears brought with them in slave vessels from the Dark Continent. To native Africans, sexual intercourse is creative and holy, allusions to it in their songs are respectful, not obscene; and the bodily movement which accompanies the performance of songs of love is not vulgar to African eyes. On the contrary, it is an artistic symbol of exalted experience.

Angel Mo' and Her Son, Roland Hayes

Amongst the Christian Negroes in America, alas, all such spontaneous musical expression was held to be debased. Hence it was neglected to the point of being lost. Only a few of our old secular folk songs exist in the South today. In my childhood I knew a considerable number of African songs, but when I went North I forgot them, and it was not until I began to meet native African musicians in Europe, many years later, that I was able to recall the old melodies laid away in the bottom drawers of my mind.

Jim Kirby probably knew more than any of us about the lore of African music. He used to say that the spirituals, the basic music of our Negro culture, were based upon recollections of African songs, and that the profane music of city Negroes was simply the familiar religious music put to swing. The sacred words were dropped, and new texts, frequently meaningless, put the burden of sensation upon the notes.

When I was a child I drank in all the music I heard: in the woods and fields; at church and singing school; in our cabin, and at the feet of my father and our friend Jim Kirby; rarely at dances, and sometimes on the dusty highroad. And so all my life was music until my father died.

It was pitiful to watch the dissolution of that strong man. I remember that his body was swollen and that he suffered horribly. He would crawl to the side of his bed and clasp the bedposts, the veins standing out from his powerful hands and wrists. Sometimes he would ask me to scratch his head with a comb, and then he would relax and grow drowsy and fall asleep. When he woke up, he would tell me a story.

For many days Pa was nearly helpless. He could not lie quietly and he could not get up out of his bed. Then, not long before he died, he seemed to recover a little. He got up and dressed and made deliveries of chairs and baskets which he had made before he was injured, carrying them out of the yard on his lame, aching back, and coming home exhausted. He had been hurt some years back, in a logging operation on Horn's Mountain, so grievously that his body could not be mended. Mother Fannie, worn with tending him and us children and our unyielding farm, put him back to bed.

Fading first and then stilled utterly, the fine, lusty voice that people stopped to listen to when he called hogs down from the Mountain; cold and quiet in death the nimble fingers that had been quick and skillful to furnish a house for his family; mercifully abated the terrifying pain, and ready for its rest the racked body. Pa died in my mother's arms.

Mr. Butler, our neighbor, measured Pa for his coffin of poplar wood. The women from the church came to sing and pray over his body. Old Ned drew his coffin to the churchyard. Behind the funeral wagon walked the population of the Flatwoods, the minister first, declaiming the sacred Scriptures; the family following, supported by relatives and friends. The faithful sang their hymns of hope and resurrection, the infidels scuffled sheepishly in the dust behind.

I saw my father die, I saw him buried. I was old enough to know that I would never see him again.

"The Lord has taken him," my mother said. That was the only explanation I had of a great and poignant mystery. I missed Pa from his place at home. I could not bear to have him gone.

CHAPTER TWO

I Worship My Mother

MOST OF what I know about my ancestors I learned from the man who owned my mother. When I went back to Georgia, in 1926, to buy the farm where Ma had lived in slavery, I found the old gentleman, the last of a great family of planters, in a shanty in Sugar Valley, six or seven miles from the Gordon County plantation which he had inherited from his father. He had been obliged to sell his property many years before, and now he lived in penury with his second wife, a nearly lifeless invalid.

The place in the hills of Gordon County used to be the summer residence of the Mann family, whose seat was down in Clayton County, south of the capital city of Atlanta. The Big House where my mother worked was not distinguished for the colonial simplicity of the manor houses built in the days of the Georges, but in my eyes, when I was a boy, it had seemed a palace. It was a commodious, two-storied structure, with wide chimneys at either end; and across the full front of it there stretched a veranda, whose roof was supported by six columns. The bedrooms gave upon a canopied balcony with an elaborately embroidered railing, its lacy scrollwork the epitome of Victorian elegance. And no slave quarters on the farm had been, on the contrary, so mean as the cabin to which the last of the Manns had been finally reduced.

Joe Mann came out into his unkempt yard to talk to me. He spoke of Pony, my mother, his first wife's favorite slave.

"You come of a great family for singin'," he said. "Do you remember that song your great-granddaddy made up? It was a song that went, 'He never said a mumberlin' word.'"

I told him I had sung that spiritual about the Crucifixion in most of the capitals of Europe, and begged him to search his memory for other recollections of my Great-grandfather Charles.

My mother and my Aunt Harriet Cross had long since told me what they knew of the legend of my first American ancestor, but Joe Mann remembered a good deal more. Charles was called something like Abá 'Ougi, out in Africa, where he had been a highborn chief. He was ambushed on the Ivory Coast, transported to Savannah, and auctioned off to a family called Weaver. That was along about 1790. It was the

I Worship My Mother

Weavers who gave my great-grandfather the Christian name of Charles and wrote out his pedigree. Then, Mr. Joe Mann reckoned, they put him to stud like a stallion.

The next summer in Paris I met Prince Oanilo, the son of the lately deposed King Behanzin of Dahomey, and Prince Tovalou, the king's nephew, and asked them if they had ever heard such a name as Joe Mann remembered my great-grandfather to have had. Prince Tovalou said that Abá was a familiar title of respect and that 'Ougi was the patronymic of the royal family of one of the tribes on the Ivory Coast.

Charles was a powerful fellow. Joe Mann said it must have taken ten men to capture him. Aboard the slaving ship, crossing the Atlantic, he lay in chains in a solitary cell. At dock in Savannah, after the other captives were driven from the ship like cattle, he strode down the gangplank alone. He was of such superior bearing, so handsome and so strong, that many plantation owners bid for his possession. The Weavers had to pay dear for him.

Although my great-grandfather never allowed his owner to become his spiritual master, he reasonably gave himself to ordered tasks on the Weaver plantation near Jonesboro, in Georgia, and it was not long before he became an overseer. It seems clear to me that he did not try to incite rebellion amongst his fellow slaves, but he did counsel them to prepare themselves against the day when God should give them their freedom. When that time came, he said, they must know how to live like free men in an alien world. He appointed secret meeting places in ravines and marshes. In the morning of the day of congregation he sowed the word across the fields. "Steal away," he would whisper to his neighbor, and the phrase was passed from mouth to mouth through all the plantations in the neighborhood. At length the ritual words were set to music and a new spiritual was born.

Charles came into contact with the doctrines and poetic images of Christianity when Northern missionaries came down to Georgia to evangelize the slaves. The apocalyptic religion of the Gospels gave him consolation, just as it had consoled the enslaved and oppressed in apostolic days. His spirit fed upon biblical promise; the Scriptures took up their residence at the tip of his tongue.

Plantation owners were reluctant to allow their slaves to attend camp meeting: they were afraid the missionaries would instruct them in the heresy of freedom. But the Negroes were determined to hear the comfortable words of Jesus and went secretly at night to sit at the feet of the Christian teachers. My great-grandfather continued to improvise musical signals to announce the

return of the preachers. Thus on a windy morning he
would sing: —

> Green trees a-bendin',
> Poor sinner stands a-tremblin',
> A trumpet sounds within-a my soul,
> I ain't got long to stay here.

Or if the meeting were prefaced by an electric storm,
he sang: —

> My Lordy calls me,
> He calls me by the thunder,
> A trumpet sounds within-a my soul,
> I ain't got long to stay here.

One night when Abá 'Ougi was himself conducting
a service on the wooded bank of the Red River, in his
capacity as self-ordained evangelist, his owner and a
company of mounted planters set out with hounds to
discover the meeting place of their slaves and put an
end, once and for all, to dread of revolution. The hounds
bayed and the Negroes scattered into the night. But
not my great-grandfather. Neither hound nor horse-
man could take him, so long as he did not sleep.

Charles spoke up to the white men, confessed that he
was shepherd to the colored Christians, and dared the
adversary to lay hands on him. Not until his companions
were safely deployed did he himself retreat into the
woods. Discovered hours later, in the deep sleep of ex-

haustion, he was captured and bound. When his captors had thus secured him, they kicked him in the face and flogged him until he was dead.

The song by which my great-granddaddy is remembered to this day, in the South, is his personal version of the story of Jesus and the Cross, a tragedy which had moved him because he, too, was a man of sorrows, and acquainted with grief.

"Wasn't it a pity an' a shame," the spiritual begins: —

> Wasn't it a pity an' a shame,
> An' He never said a mumberlin' word,
> Wasn't it a pity an' a shame,
> An' He never said a mumberlin' word, oh,
> Not a word, not a word, not a word!
> Dey nailed Him to the tree,
> An' He never said a mumberlin' word,
> Dey nailed Him to the tree,
> An' He never said a mumberlin' word, oh,
> Not a word, not a word, not a word!
>
> Dey pierced Him in the side,
> In-a-the side, in-a-the side,
> Dey pierced Him in the side,
> In-a-the side, in-a-the side,
> De blood came a-twinkalin' down
> An' He never said a mumberlin' word,
> The blood came a-twinkalin' down
> An' He never said a mumberlin' word, oh,
> Not a word, not a word, not a word!

I Worship My Mother

He bow'd His head an' died
An' He never said a mumberlin' word,
He bow'd His head an' died
An' He never said a mumberlin' word, oh,
Not a word, not a word, not a word!

In 1921, at tea in the London house of Stephen Graham, whose book about American Negroes, *Children of the Slaves*, was newly published, I sang the "Crucifixion" in the form in which I had learned it from my mother. The Reverend Hugh B. Chapman heard me there and invited me to sing it in the Royal Chapel of the Savoy. A few weeks later I sang my royal African ancestor's music to their Britannic Majesties, King George and Queen Mary, at Buckingham Palace.

It interested me to recall, after I was commanded to sing before King George V, that my great-grandfather had been sold into slavery in an American state named for the second of the British Georges. Georgia, the last chartered colony in North America, had been planned as a kind of buffer state between the earlier colonies and Spanish Florida. New forms of agriculture were to have been introduced there, with hired labor instead of slaves. The first Georgian settlement was made in Savannah, in 1733, by British Nonconformists, German Lutherans, Piedmontese Protestants, Scotch Calvinists, sectarian Swiss and Portuguese, and Continental Jews — a miscellaneous company assembled by James Edward Oglethorpe, a philanthropic Member of Parliament who, after distinguishing himself in the war against the Turks, took up the cause of Abolition.

In a hurry to spend a parliamentary provision of some ten thousand pounds, the colonists, many of them penniless debtors, straightway planted vineyards, mulberry trees, medicinal herbs and henequen. The vines and the trees and the plants withered under the hot Georgia sun. The colonists applied for help from experienced agriculturists in Virginia and the Carolinas, who promised to lend a hand provided they should be furnished with a complement of slaves. Accordingly, in 1749, slaves were imported, immigration from the older colonies set in, rum was offered for sale, and in 1753 Georgia became a royal province under a new charter. Except for the Yankee Parish of St. John, which had been settled by New Englanders from Dorchester, Massachusetts, the climate of the colony was prevailingly Loyalist, up to the Revolution.

Cherokee Indians, migrants of Iroquois stock, were in possession of the hill country in the northern part of the new colony. Once they had ranged over the whole territory now divided by Virginia, Tennessee, the Carolinas, Alabama and Georgia; but by the end of the eighteenth century they had been crowded into the narrow limits of a few counties in the northwestern part of Georgia, where they made their capital at New Echota, a few miles from the farm where I was born.

There the Indians learned to cultivate the soil, to spin and weave. Moravian missionaries established churches and schools amongst them. The family letters of a lady from Boston, the white wife of a New Echota Indian, testify to the growth of a settled culture there, pious and literate, and not without traces of elegance. But in the year 1802 the Georgia colonists offered to cede to the Federal Government that part of their royal grant now known as Alabama and Mississippi in return for the Cherokee territory. Anglo-Saxon settlers from southern Georgia, anxious to dissociate themselves from "foreigners," began at once to press on into the Indian country, and by demand of these invaders the national government, after more than thirty years of wavering, sent General Winfield Scott and seven thousand soldiers to New Echota. The Indian inhabitants were driven from their homes.

Amongst the white newcomers to the Cherokee country was the family of Edward Mann, who had bought my Grandfather Peter, the son of Charles, from the Weavers down in Jonesboro. In the early summer of every year Ed Mann, Joe's father, made the annual hegira with his entourage to the hills of Gordon County, where his slaves, amongst them Granddaddy Peter, opened the new farm to the plow.

On the day of my grandfather's birth — according to the family history — my Great-grandfather Charles lifted the child up from his mother's arms, laid him silently down again, dropped to his knees, and buried his head in his hands.

"I was born a free man," he said. "My son comes into the world a slave."

Grandfather Peter Weaver grew up to be a fine, strong man, and when he turned twenty he began to pay court to Mandy Mann, over on a neighboring plantation. Although stout Negro bucks were commonly bred out, to increase the stock, the Manns and the Weavers agreed that Peter and Mandy should be allowed to have a Christian marriage. To this end, one of them had to be sold. Ed Mann paid fifteen hundred dollars for Peter and married him up to his own slave girl Mandy, the daughter of black Jesse Mann and his Indian wife. Grandmaw Mandy was a tall, copper-colored woman, with straight black hair. I am said to take after Peter, while my brother Robert is the spitting image of Mandy.

By the time the Mann plantations descended to Joseph Mann, Peter and Mandy had five children: Fannie (my mother), Aunt Harriet, Uncle Robert (my wife's father), Uncle Wiltsie, and Uncle Simon, all of whom took the surname Mann after the Liberation. Joe Mann never liked my Grandfather Peter, who was clearly difficult to discipline. One day, during the War Between the States, he ordered him to cross his hands — a warning that a beating was about to be administered — and when my grandfather refused to stand up to the rawhide whip, Joe threatened to kill him. Peter ran away to the woods, where he lived for eighteen months, returning now and again to his cabin, but otherwise dependent upon food cached in trees by his friends.

Peter usually carried a bottle of scent killer in his pocket, so that if hounds were put on his trail he could put them off again. But one night, during a visit to the plantation, he was warned that he had not a minute to lose if he valued his life. Joe Mann was going to set the dogs on him instanter. He leaped from the cabin in his nightshirt and ran for safety towards the undisclosing waters of the Oostanaula — leaving his bottle of magical oil behind. Before he reached the riverbank, the dogs had picked up his ineradicable odor and run him up a tree. Joe Mann rode up after the hounds and ordered Peter down, promising safe convoy to the farm. But when they got back, he tied him up, and punctuated with his whip a morbid history of all of

Peter's memorable acts of disobedience. My grand-father never recovered from the beating he took. He died before the Surrender.

When the Yankees came, Joe Mann was naturally re-luctant to meet them. He ran away and hid in the woods near his Jonesboro plantation until the war was over. After the Liberation, when he could safely re-turn to his house, he called his slaves together and told them they were free. He offered shelter to those who were willing to work on shares, and liberty to those who wished to move on. Grandmaw Mandy, who wanted to give her children an education, set out with them on the road to Atlanta, where they met up with a caravan of freemen on their way to Tennessee.

Mother Fannie had been pantrymaid in the Big House before her promotion to be lady's maid to Mrs. Mann, and it was in the pantry, oddly enough, that she acquired the taste for learning that her mother intended to satisfy. When the Mann children came to her for bread and molasses after school, she would ask them to recite their lessons to her. They showed her their schoolbooks and sounded out mysterious printed words, symbols of scholarship to those who could recognize them. My mother wanted more than anything to go to school herself. She would have liked to be a teacher of Negro children. She was cruelly disillusioned when my father turned out to be illiterate himself and unsympathetic with her appetite for book-learning.

Grandmaw Mandy and her daughter Pony, my mother, ate abundantly of the bread of suffering all their lives. Both were schooled in bearing pain and disappointment, whether from the hand of destiny, which they respected, or from some more humanly vagarious source.

One day my mother was sitting in her pantry, repairing a dress for her mistress and waiting for the children to come for their afternoon lunch. She had laid out a loaf of bread for them, and a bowl of brown sugar. Her master, passing through the pantry, stopped to say, "Pony, what you doing here?"

"Sewing, Marse Joe," said my mother.

"You're a liar," said Joe, flicking his whip in her direction. "You are stealing my sugar."

"I ain't doing no such thing, Marse Joe," she protested.

"Maybe a good whupping will make you tell the truth," he said, wherewith he thrashed her soundly.

Mrs. Mann appeared upon the scene and begged my mother to confess, to save her skin, that she had stolen some sugar.

"Yes, Marse Joe, I did steal some sugar," said my mother at last.

Angel Mo' and Her Son, Roland Hayes

"I know you did, you wicked girl," said Mr. Mann, "and now I shall whup you for telling me lies."

Grandmaw Mandy had her tribulations, too. The Manns were up in Gordon County when news arrived that Sherman was on the march. Joe Mann ordered a hasty return to the Jonesboro place. My grandmother, being with child, was fearful of the wagon journey. The master lost his temper when she asked to be left behind. He threw her into a tub of cold water. Something thereby happened to her ears, she always said, and at the time I knew her she was as deaf as a stone.

II

Not long after my mother's marriage, it became apparent to her that Pa could not support a family of children in Chattanooga. She longed to return to Gordon County to claim, if she could, Grandmaw's sharecropping portion of the old place; but it took her nearly ten years to persuade my father to go back to the farm. My brother William and my sister Mattie were still hardly more than babies then, and Ma bundled them up and took them down to the Flatwoods. The plantation had been divided up, but Mose Garlington agreed to sell her ten acres which had once belonged to the Manns. There, in the cabin which Pa built and furnished, the rest of us children were born.

I Worship My Mother

Mother Fannie worked hard on the farm. Indeed, she worked hard all her life. She plowed and hoed and picked cotton. She washed and ironed for the white families in the neighborhood, the Gordons and the Manns and Squire Kemp, who kept the store and owned the sawmill and gristmill in Little Row. Years later, when I was in England, she wrote to me from Boston that her life on the farm had seemed a constant repetition of an endless journey between house and barn and cotton gin. She had never expected to see in this world, she said, what she had seen with me. For all the years of my childhood she had no rest from labor, except for going to church.

When my mother went back home in 1875, there was no meetinghouse nearer than the white folks' Baptist Church in West Union, about five miles from the farm. Every Sunday Ma and Aunt Maria Mann walked back and forth between the Flatwoods and West Union, where they took such comfort as they could from their places in the back pew. As soon as I was able to walk so far, I went to meeting with them. My first intimation of the great gulf fixed between white people and black came to me when I was very small. I used to wonder — although I cannot remember that I ever really inquired — why my mother and my Aunt Maria and I always sat on a bench so far from the preacher.

Angel Mo' and Her Son, Roland Hayes

I was about six years old, I think, when my mother and my aunt founded Mount Zion Baptist Church in the Flatwoods and gave the Negroes their own spiritual home. My mother, as we children grew older, tried to temper the difference between white and black. She had lived in the city long enough to know that black people had always to appease the white, no matter where they lived. She was gentler than my Aunt Maria, who hated to take a back seat for anybody.

"If white people wants to come to dis church in de Flatwoods," she said, "let dem take de back seat amongst us." She was the better reconciled to the practice of segregation because it seemed to her, she said, that the white folks' preachers preached too much about hell and too little about heaven.

Ma hoped that I would grow up to be a preacher, and if I failed to realize her ambition for me, it was not because my religious education was neglected. After the colored families had their own church, I think I did not miss a single service in it so long as we lived on the farm.

We had neither Prayer Book nor hymnal in the Mount Zion Church. Printed books were too dear. We had a kind of local ritual, however, subject to variation at the hands of itinerant preachers and revivalists who visited us. Service always began, for example, with a hymn which the deacon lined out, two verses at a time: —

> Amazing grace, how sweet the sound
> That saved a wretch like me.

When we had sung so far, he would line out another pair: —

> I once was lost, but now I'm found,
> Was blind, but now I see.

With what a joyous burst of song we repeated these evangelical stanzas, set to tunes that everybody knew! Prayers and Scripture reading led at length up to the dramatic climax of the meeting, the pastor's sermon.

Sometimes the preacher sang his homily, and then my little body could hardly contain my heart. I absorbed it word by word and note by note, so that I could repeat it at home and in the field. Such a sermon in song is an Old Testament narrative which I believe has been sung in concert halls only by me. It came to be known as "The Fourth Dimension": —

> Now look at brother Jonah,
> A servant of the Lord,
> Was commanded by the God of Peace
> To go to Nineveh to prophesy.

(49)

Angel Mo' and Her Son, Roland Hayes

My God is so high you can't get over Him,
He's so low you can't get under Him,
He's so wide that you can't get around Him.
You must come in by and through the Lamb.

Another great favorite was a sermon about Ezekiel,
in the singing of which the congregation had learned
to take the part of a kind of Greek chorus. The preacher
sang: —

God told Ezekiel by his words,
"Go down and prophesy."
Ezekiel prophesied by the power of God,
Commanded the bones to arise.

The congregation then demanded: "How did the bones
get together with the leg bone?" Whereupon the
preacher explained: —

Ezekiel said, "The toe bone connected with the foot bone,
The foot bone connected with the ankle bone,
The ankle bone connected with the knee bone,
The knee bone connected with the thigh bone.

"They walked all around,
Dry bones.
They walked around together,
Dry bones.
Why don't you rise and hear the word of the Lord?"

The congregation then inquires: "How did the head
bone get together with the thigh bone?"

I Worship My Mother

Ezekiel said [intones the preacher], "The thigh bone con-
nected with the hip bone,
The hip bone connected with the back bone,
The back bone connected with the neck bone,
And the neck bone connected with the head bone."

This sermon, "Ye Dry Bones Goin' to Rise Again,"
was first preached to us by our own pastor, a powerful black man, the Reverend Charles Foster, who had
a thrilling voice and used to stay amongst us for two
or three weeks at a time. He had an amazing repertoire
of Biblical paraphrases: "The Horse Pawing in the
Valley," "The Sun Do Move," and an epic piece about
the Creation. We knew his sermons by name and called
for them over and over again. After the sermon, the
preacher and the congregation sang spirituals until
everybody was worn out. As poor as the people of our
neighborhood were, they showered Brother Foster with
donations — eggs and chickens and fine smoked hams
and bacon — whenever he left us to return to his home
in Rome.

It became my duty in the church, as I grew older
and less timid, to learn new songs and teach them to
the congregation. It was in this oral fashion that the
spirituals were handed down amongst Negroes everywhere, and thus they have traveled all over the South.
Hundreds of variations have been created because the

texts were rarely written down. I have always used in my concerts the Flatwoods version of songs I knew in my childhood. Every year I sing spirituals which are new to my programs, and nearly always they have come from the neighborhood of Curryville.

As lately as the summer of 1941, while I was visiting my farm with my wife and my daughter, Africa, I heard a workman humming the strains of a song which I had long since known and forgotten. The tune went through my head for many days, and little by little the words came back. I remembered that it had been sung in our countryside by a woman of both African and Indian blood. The music is likewise both African and Indian, but the culmination of the melody is composed of purely African tones and rhythms. The text is something like this: —

> Ise moughty tired of dis heavy load,
> Ah wanna be wid Jedus
>   In Sodom and Gomorrah.
> Oh take me ober Jerdon
> To my Jedus' campground.

We children grew up with the language of the Bible ever in our ears. In church it struck me that the scriptural words were often warm and comfortable. At home we were more likely to hear the hard sayings of Jesus and the Prophets. In later years my mother used

to repeat Jesus' words of consolation, like: "Come
unto me, all ye that labour and are heavy laden, and I
will give you rest." But when we were children, she
was more likely to instruct us in harder doctrine.

Mother Fannie believed in perfection. "Be ye therefore perfect, even as your Father which is in heaven is
perfect." She believed it was possible for Christian people, through grace, actually to become perfect. Indeed,
she thought they were under obligation to achieve perfection. The severest and most ascetic sayings of Jesus
— Ma's versions of them were sometimes, I dare say,
apocryphal — were always on her mind and heart. If
she learned, for example, that my older brothers had
been seeing worldly companions, she would repeat,
through narrowed lips, a verse I have never quite been
able to identify: "Jesus said, 'Come out from amongst
them.' " Perhaps she was a little harder on us small
sinners than her Master would have been, but she was
unwilling to take chances with our immortal souls. She
used to tell us that we could not run with sinners and
be pure ourselves.

When we were children our venerable mother sometimes seemed cold and hard. She was never unkind, she
was never unjust. She simply was thoroughly persuaded
of the difference between right and wrong, and she
steadfastly refused to relax her moral judgments. My

older brothers, if they found her discipline unbearable, took to running away from home. It was hard for us to understand why Ma, who was so jolly when there was no wrong in sight, should be so much more severe with her own children than she was with outsiders.

I remember seeing my mother cry only once, and that was when my sister Mattie, her only daughter, died; and to me, who grew steadily more and more dependent upon the solid rock of her character, she was soft and warm only once. The last time I saw her she broke through her devout reserve for a single moment, after more than fifteen years of resistance to my vocation, and said, "Son, you are the continuation of me."

My mother was a small, slight woman, with a beautiful, erect carriage which hard work never bent. She was very little more than five feet tall, and she moved rapidly about on her small feet, quick and sprightly as a bird. Her facial structure was both delicate and strong, and you could see from her sharp, keen eyes that she was able to penetrate a situation in an instant. Her skin was as smooth as an olive.

On weekdays she wore plain ginghams and printed calicos, which she herself made up on lines which were perhaps more practical than fashionable. Her "common-sense" shoes, laced tightly to support her ankles, reached up to the hem of her skirt. On Sundays she dressed like an immaculate deaconess in a good, black-calico frock, over which she wore a starched white apron. A white ruffled bonnet and high buttoned shoes of soft kid completed the dominical costume. I was proud of her when we went to church together.

III

Next to our souls, Mother Fannie cherished our minds. She wanted us to have an education so that we could do good in the world. She was distressed by the meager provision made for the free education of Negro children in our county. It could not have been that we were neglected by the county school board for the reason that we were too numerous to be accommodated economically, because we were barely one in seven of the whole number of children of school age. Yet in the Flatwoods we went to school not more than three or four months in the year, for seven years at the most. My brother Willie, who taught in our school for a term or two, received a salary of fifteen dollars a month.

It is recorded in Miss Lulie Pitts's *History of Gordon County* that in 1899, our last year on the farm, one fifth of the local colored children did not go to school at all. The rest of us kept the winter term in January, February, and March. In the summertime most of us had to work in the fields. Perhaps it would have been scarcely worth while to supply us with the midsummer term with which the white children rounded out a school year of five months. At any rate, it was my mother and not I who complained of the brevity of our seasons of schooling.

How I hated my school days in the Flatwoods! On Friday afternoons we had rhetoricals, which I regularly began to anticipate with anguish on Monday. On the Friday of my first week at school the teacher asked me to recite a simple rhymed couplet. I became sick to my stomach and asked leave to go home. Ma met me at the door of our cabin and asked me what was the matter. I said I was sick. She took me by the hand, without so much as a word, and marched me back to the schoolhouse, where she sat stiffly on a bench until the rhetorical was over. She even tried to make me recite the poem, but I was unable to stand up on my feet, I could not speak. I was scared into insensibility. When I see my brother's children take cover today, like frightened baby deer, I am reminded of my childhood. Until I was nearly grown up, shyness and timidity seemed to wax with the years. Fright turned into morbid melancholy. If somebody spoke to me directly, I broke down and cried.

In the third grade I had the good fortune to sit under

a respectably educated teacher, a graduate of the Atlanta Baptist College, by the name of Wilkin Green. Mr. Green took me in hand. He appealed to my pride by praising the little efforts I could make to take my place in the life of the school. He told me fascinating stories about great men of our race: about Pierre-Dominique Toussaint L'Ouverture, for example, the liberator of Haiti, a descendant of an African chief. I learned a poem about this valorous man — how he got his name by forcing a gap in the ranks of the enemy; how he went over to the French to help them free the slaves; how he became the "Bonaparte of San Domingo"; and finally, captured by the army he had renounced for empire, how he died in the prison of Joux. I recited that poem in all the colored schools in the county.

I cannot say that I have ever outgrown my timidities entirely. In fact, I have come to believe that shyness is not a wholly undesirable quality in people who must appear frequently before the public. I have often felt embarrassed before some vast new audience, and yet have been compensated by the emotional toning up which follows an effort to overcome nervousness. Perhaps the bashful man who learns to control his diffidence is the man who in the long run can do the most unlikely things.

After my father's death in 1898, when I was eleven

years old, my brother Robert and I were obliged to leave school and go to work. Our mother could no longer keep the family together singlehanded. She was exhausted from the strain of my father's long illness, although I must praise her for bearing herself so proudly and bravely when he died and was buried. I did not see her break down as she did when Mattie died. She seemed to take Pa's death more calmly, as later, full of years, she spoke with serenity of her own approaching death. Like a good countrywoman she naturally related death and the passing years, and like an evangelical Christian she was full of high hope for the life eternal.

I walked with her up the lane to Mount Zion Church, behind my father's coffin, and I heard her voice ring out clearly, even exultantly, when she joined the mourners' chorus in that triumphant song of faith, "Roun' about de Mountain": —

> Roun' about de mountain,
> Roun' about de mountain,
> My God's a-rulin' an' he'll
> Rise in His arm.

> The Lord loves a sinner,
> The Lord loves a sinner man,
> The Lord loves a sinner,
> An' he'll rise in His arm.

I Worship My Mother

When I was a sinner, a-seekin' jes' like you,
I went down in the valley,
I prayed till I come through.

You hypocrite, you concubine,
You're placed amongst the swine,
You go to God with your liver an' tongue,
But you leave your heart behin'.

    The Lord loves a sinner,
    The Lord loves a sinner man,
    The Lord loves a sinner,
    An' he'll rise in His arm.

I'm goin' roun' the mountain,
There I'll take-a my stand.
I heard the voice of Jesus,
Thank God it's in this land.

    The Lord loves a sinner,
    The Lord loves a sinner man,
    The Lord loves a sinner,
    An' he'll rise in His arm.

Roun' about de mountain,
Roun' about de mountain,
My God's a-rulin' an' he'll
Rise in His arm.

The funeral past and done, Ma took stock of our condition. She calculated that it would be a good two years of hard work for all of us, before we could pay off the debts which had accumulated while Pa was sick. Then she could take us to the city for the serious business of getting us an education for life.

Ma hired an additional piece of land from Babe Hendricks, across the lane from the home farm. Robert and I burned it off and planted it on shares. I learned to plow in that field. One day I plowed into a nest of yellow jackets. I thought I was afire. I thought I should perish before I could get home to my mother. Burning and swollen and bandaged, I reflected that the sociable nature of those insects, whose habits I had studied in school, was not to be counted on outside of books.

In a field on Babe Hendricks's own place, where I worked for wages when I was not busy at home, my mother one day caught me preaching to Molly, a blind horse we had bought after Ned, our old ox, died. Ma must have been sorely torn between mystical inclination and moral duty. At any rate, she heard me out, all the way through the "Dry Bones" sermon; and then she came out from her hiding place behind a cornstack.

"Son," she said, "I am glad to hear you singin' all dem Bible words. I'm glad you listen to what de preacher says in church. Now get along to your work, and try to earn yo' fifty cents."

It was also my job to fetch and deliver the washing

which Ma did for three or four white families in the neighborhood. I dreaded the days when I had to visit John Gordon's house. Mr. Gordon, who kept a stable of fine horses and a pack of hounds, always carried a long whip which he used to crack around my ankles, whilst pretending to sic his dogs on me. I had often heard Mose Garlington describe the flogging of slaves, back in the days before the Surrender, and from the tip of John Gordon's whip I got my first taste of what rawhide had meant to my forebears.

Sometime after I returned to Georgia to take up farming in the 1930's, Mr. Gordon, who then owned a hardware store in Calhoun, called on me in my house, the very same house, except for renovation, that he had lived in when I was a boy. He recalled the days when I used to carry the clean linen up to his house on the hill, and stop on — infrequently — to play with his daughter; but we did not speak of the times he had frightened me with his whip and his hounds.

After Pa died, there were times when we desperately needed meat and flour and had no money in the house to pay for them. Then Mother would borrow from Ben Gordon, John's kinsman, and sign a paper which required her to make repayment, with heavy interest, in the work of her hands or in crops at the time of gathering. It was a bad moment when Ned died, because we had to buy blind Molly on credit. Ma took over the care of our own fields then, and Robert and I went to work for cash wages.

And so my brother and I, breadwinners now, entered our teens. So modest my mother was, and reticent, that we were nowise prepared for our approach to maturity. We had learned something about life from nature, but if as small children we talked, for example, about the mating of chickens, we were hushed up. We were not allowed to speak of such things.

Our last year on the farm was an especially critical time for me, with Pa dead and my older brothers away from home. A precocious cousin of exactly my age used to tell me, with a gleam in his eye, about the romantic adventures of his older brothers. His sordid stories lingered in my mind in place of sound knowledge. My cousin warned me that to approach my elders for an explanation of these matters was only to court a cuff or a whipping. All through my adolescence I wanted to plunge myself into the ground at any mention of sexual experience. A thin, frail little colored boy, full of queer feelings and emotionally separate, I thought of my body with anxiety and fear, and tried to comfort myself with music and religion.

It was at that time, although I could not confide everything to her, that I began to think of my mother as a tower of strength. If she was severe, she was also righteous and strong, and I leaned upon her strength. I needed then and later — although I do not profess always to have understood that need — not kindness so much as discipline. Many a peremptory rebuff lay ahead of me. I needed in my later life the support of steel. Feathers might have consoled me in my childhood, but they would not have helped me to become a man. I was a timid, perplexed, uneducated Negro boy. I had to learn to be a man in a world in which privilege is reserved for children of a different complexion.

CHAPTER THREE

I Leave the Farm

M Y WIFE, who was born Alzada Mann, remembers me in my first pair of fancy shoes. I was fourteen years old and my shoes were bright yellow. They squeaked in a high-pitched voice which gratified my ears. I was "as bragge and as proude as a pecocke" to wear them every day. Down on the farm we had worn shoes only in winter. In the late fall, after the cotton was sold, Ma used to buy brass-tipped brogans to keep our feet warm until spring. In summer we wore them only on Sundays, and even then we walked barefoot up Mount Zion Lane until we came within sight of the steeple. There we plunged into the woods and put on our brogans and clumped impressively into the church. Many of our friends had no shoes at all.

In the fall of 1900 we had no shoes ourselves. We paid our debts in the Flatwoods and went to Chattanooga with the little cash money Ma had left after the last crop gathering. Robert and I went barefoot, summer style.

I Leave the Farm

Mother and Baby Jesse took the train up to the city, while Robert and I went over the road with Frank Adams. Frank had a horse and wagon and was moving up to Chattanooga because he could no longer put up with the Flatwoods wits. He had an infantine lisp which stimulated his friends' gift of imitancy; and when he became guilty of the additional folly of marrying a notorious woman, life became much too difficult for him at home. He had been long accustomed to the simple mimicry of his faltering articulation, but now his friends were lisping lewd commentaries on his bride. Hence he struck out to the city, where he hoped to live in peace.

I am surprised, now that I think of it, that Ma let us accompany Frank and his ambiguous lady on the two-day journey from down country. I suppose she felt sorry for him. She would not thus have exposed us for any advantage accruing to herself.

Robert and I took turns riding old moon-eyed Molly, who pulled a load of furniture and feed in our own one-horse cart. Although Molly could see a little in the dead of night, she was as blind as a barn-owl in the day-time. Whoever drove her had to keep her on the right side of the road, while the other of us, traveling on foot, urged our cow along. The cow was securely tied to the wagon, but she was not used to traveling thirty-five miles a day and she needed frequent encouragement.

We were very nearly done out of that cow when we got to the city, come to think of it. An innocent-looking old black man offered to take her over in exchange for an animal that was supposed to be already conditioned to urban life, and we were saved from a costly mistake only by my Aunt Harriet's intuition.

"Look out for that thar cow," she warned us. "She looks like she can mos' kick de moon."

Aunt Harriet Cross had invited us all to come and stay with her in the colored section around Tenth and Douglas. Robert and I were a good ten miles from her house when the sun went down on the second day of our journey. We had barely reached the southern end of Chickamauga Park. Frank and his wife decided to make camp, but Robert was determined to go on, arguing that it was now dark enough for Molly to see a little piece of the road in front of her.

At ten o'clock we reached the brightly lighted streets of Chattanooga. Now I may say that I have visited practically all of the great cities of Europe since that time, but not one of them has ever held the wonder for me of that first view of the Southern city, the breathless and holy wonder of a revelation. Perched up on Molly, with Robert afoot by my side, I rode through the gas-lit avenues of a New Jerusalem.

I Leave the Farm

Aunt Harriet and her husband, my Uncle Cross, received our family most hospitably. Uncle Cross, a huckster, had a reputation for being able to skin a housewife out of her eyeballs, but he had nothing but kindness for us. Aunt Harriet was my mother's own sister, and their brother Robert, for whom my brother was named, likewise lived in Chattanooga, in one of the remoter colored quarters. Uncle Robert had a good many children, of whom Alzada was one, and Brother Robert and I were anxious to meet them. Accordingly Ma bought us each a new pair of shoes and we went out to the eastern outskirts of the city, one Sunday, to pay a visit to our cousins. That was the day I met my wife, although she pretends now that it was my shoes and not my person that impressed her then.

We were all anxious to have a home of our own as soon as we were able. I got a job, Mother took in washing, and presently we rented a house on Douglas Street, not far from Aunt Harriet's. Robert and Jesse went to school and Ma promised me that in a year or so I should have my turn at book-learning. Robert was two years older than I, but he was in delicate health. Just before my fourteenth birthday I therefore became the wage-earning head of a family of four, with a fine position in the Price and Evans Sashweight Foundry at eighty cents a day.

Angel Mo' and Her Son, Roland Hayes

When I applied for a job the foreman said, "Son, you're moughty small. Do you think you can do a man's work?" I said I had a mother and two brothers to support and I reckoned I could do anything.

The foreman put me right to work with a wheelbarrow, along with a full-grown man. From early morning until three o'clock that afternoon we unloaded scrap iron from freight cars and wheeled it into the foundry. Then we went to work for the rest of the day at the cupola, where scrap iron and pig iron were melted for casting. We set the fires and plied the furnace with wood. When the iron was melted we tapped the cupola and let the sputtering liquid metal run out into a mortar-lined steel ladle, from which my partner and I distributed it amongst the molders by means of small hand ladles. That was our work every day thereafter. I carry today on my feet and legs the scars of many a burn from molten iron, which had the habit of exploding in every direction when it was spilled out upon the damp earth. Time and again my flesh was burned to the bone.

At length I was given a chance to learn the trade of core making. A core is a molded form which is used to make an opening in an otherwise solid casting. It is made from a tricky blend of sand, resin and sticky black molasses, and even today it is molded by hand.

I Leave the Farm

I learned to make the cores which form the holes in old-fashioned window-sash weights. Every hole in every weight in every window in the world has required its own separate core, and I have made hundreds of thousands of them.

Core making was easier than the carrier's job. I had shorter hours and better pay, and plenty of time for experimentation. I discovered an efficient new formula for blending, and then I was promoted to be foreman of my shop. My wages went up all at once to five dollars a day. I hired a couple of Negro boys to help me, out of my own pay, and when the day's supply of cores was made I was free to go home. In my sixteenth year I went back to school, in the third grade. I could go only to afternoon classes, but I paid my teacher to tutor me after school.

That year was a turning point in my life. A triad of events reshaped my destiny. An ungainly full-grown boy by then, with muscles of steel and a man's habit of work, I began my formal education in the company of infants. In the same year I was dragged through a conveyor belt and sent for many weeks to bed, more dead than alive. And I was still not quite sixteen when I was converted to true religion and baptized by immersion into running water.

Aunt Harriet had taken us, when we were fresh

from the country, to the First African Baptist Church, most of whose parishioners were stylish colored people with straight hair and store clothes. We felt loutish, out of place, unwelcome. When Robert began to take piano lessons from Mrs. Kennedy, the organist of the Monumental Baptist Church, he heard that the congregation there was composed of less feverish inhabitants of the colored quarter. So when we left Aunt Harriet's roof and were at liberty as well to leave her church, we found ourselves happy in a new spiritual home. There was no "Hoity-toity! Madam-is-in-her-airs" amongst the Monumental Baptists.

In 1902 there came to town a celebrated zealot, the Reverend Mr. Ward, a persuasive Negro evangelist, and I gave myself to Jesus. That was a long time ago. I confess that I no longer go regularly to church to meet my Lord, nor do I now believe my God to be precisely the deity of ecumenical doctrine. Still, in those days, the Jesus of my mother's religion was truly my Lord and my Redeemer. I was ready to abandon and renounce the world for Him. It may be thought, since Ma had allowed us so little liberty, that I did not actually have anything much to surrender in this world. Perhaps I had to give up vain hope and boyish desire rather than fixed habit and worldly custom. Yet such as my attachments were, I gave them readily up to follow Him.

I made my public confession of faith at the end of an evening of fervent sermonizing and heart-warming singing. The congregation sang two spirituals which never failed to induce the surrender of some questing soul: "What Will You Say When You Come to Meet Your Lord?" and "There's No Hiding Place Down There." It was in my mind, as I approached the sinners' bench, that I should have to give up, above all, my unconverted companions; and if I did not immediately renounce all my friends who were not church boys, I forthwith explained to them that I expected them to behave like church boys when they were with me.

I was baptized in the Tennessee River. A day or two after my conversion, I was force-marched across the city in angelic habit, together with twenty-five or thirty heterogeneous fellow converts, and led down to the river's edge, where I received the watery seal of my profession. I was baptized into Christ Jesus, into His death. I came out of the water ready to walk in newness of life. Ma said, when we went home together, "Now, son, you must come out from amongst them."

My first act of renunciation was to give up buck-and-wing dancing, in which I had only lately become

proficient. My legs still hold the memory of the steps
of the buck and wing and I dare say that even now I
could execute them accurately. Still, except for that
boyish surrender, my need for music might never have
become a mission. If I couldn't make music with my
feet, I had to learn to let it come out of my mouth
like a Christian.

Neither my mother nor the compulsions of my religion required me to withdraw from a quartet which
I had joined. Our songs, to be sure, were sometimes subject to revision in the interest of piety, but so long as
I went home by half-past nine at night and refrained
from street dancing and other low forms of minstrelsy,
Ma allowed me to remain in that profitable organization.

Robert Igoe, who sang second tenor in our curbstone quartet, was a handsome boy, in an Indian sort
of way, and had a fine leading voice. He became a baker
and married one of my cousins, Aunt Harriet's daughter.
I sometimes see him when I go up from the farm to
Chattanooga, where he still goes about making music.
My brother Robert sang the bass, a boy by the name of
Ben Ingram the baritone, and I sang tenor voice. We
called ourselves the Silver-Toned Quartet and soon
graduated from the curbstone to the railway station,
where we sang at the arrival and departure of late-
afternoon and evening trains. In the summertime we

strolled up and down the avenues where rich people sat on their verandas to enjoy the night air, and caught in our caps the nickels, dimes and quarters they shelled out to us over the hedges.

Our harmonies were personal discoveries, although a good deal of our musical improvisation perhaps was illegitimate. Sometimes we imitated the minstrel singers with whose harmonizations my ear had become familiar before I "came out from amongst them": going from the tonic chord into the minor mode, thence into a deep minor and back into the major. Barbershop harmony, if you will, but good practice for the ear. When we got into bad musical habits we stood a good chance of having them corrected in the choir of the Monumental Baptist Church.

The boys of our neighborhood had an evening rendezvous on the sidewalk in front of the Fort Wood grocery store, and I used to listen there, entranced, to one of the older boys, Lemus Hardison, who sang soft and low in a high, sweet voice. I knew nothing then of the middle voice, or *mezza voce*, although I had unconsciously acquired the first principles of its use from my father; but I said to myself that I wanted to be able to sing like that, to sing with beauty. It had always been as natural for me to sing as for water to bubble up out of a spring, but now it came to me that the voice possessed certain delightful qualities that only practice and experimentation could release. I began to apply myself to the cultivation of those qualities so that, like Lemus, I could sing beautifully.

II

At the time of my conversion I was working in the Case and Hedges Foundry. On the day after my baptism I went to the shop, all tired out, and took my customary place in front of a set of rattles fastened to an endless belt. It was my job to fill the rattles — a kind of iron basket — with newly cast pipe fittings. The fittings were cleaned and polished by friction — it is called "tumbling" in professional circles — during their course along the conveyor, and at the end of the chain they were automatically dumped out. The rattles were returned, bottom side up, on the underside of a revolving belt to the point where I stood beside a truck filled with unpolished fittings.

I had just loaded one of the rattles, and was ready to throw the conveyor belt on with a stick, when I saw that the idler had flopped off from the governor and was revolving ineffectually. I tried to replace the idler with my stick, which was then and there caught up in the twisting loop of leather; and before I could let go my grasp on it, I found myself being pulled into an

(74)

insensible machine which had been put in motion by the contraction of the idler. Hand, arm, shoulder, and then my whole body, were drawn ineluctably into an engine of indescribable torture.

Crushed between the conveyor belt and the pulley which powered it, I went around and around, through three revolutions of the pulley, before the engine attendant saw me and shut off the motor. By that time I was mashed flat and badly lacerated, but I was also mercifully unconscious.

I came to in a plaster cast in my bed at home. Negroes were rarely hospitalized in those days, but I had received first aid at the plant, and then I was taken home in an ambulance. My mother told me afterwards that when she saw me carried into the house, bound up like a mummy, she had run hysterically out to the kitchen lest she should hear that I was dead. I was secretly comforted to know that she had been so nearly overcome with an emotional feeling which she would have been reluctant to show to me more immediately.

The company provided an attendant to help Ma look after me, and during my convalescence a company officer came to offer me a job for life. He thought I might like to work as a yard foreman, with only paper work to do, but Ma agreed with me that I should not try to make capital out of my injuries. Instead, I said

Angel Mo' and Her Son, Roland Hayes

I would come back to work at my old job. As soon as I was able, I went back to the shop, only to find that I could not stand the sight of rattles and conveyors any longer. When I saw the machine in operation again, I could not understand how I had come out of it alive. I quite simply believed that my escape was miraculous. God had spared me, I thought, to work out in me some mission which had begun with my baptism. I have never entirely lost, since that time, the feeling that I have had a heavenly vocation to fulfill, although I did not know then that I should make a ministry of music.

After my sixteenth birthday it was Robert's turn to go to work, and I entered the fifth grade as a regular pupil. It was embarrassing to have to make recitations in front of children so much younger than I and so much more used to reading aloud and reciting. I could read the books and write a fair hand as well as any sixth-grader, but I was slow in arithmetic. My teacher, Mrs. Cora Phillips, a motherly woman, was kind to me. Like Mr. Green, she praised me for what I could do by myself, and helped me with difficult studies. I had a good literal memory, so that I was sometimes enabled to repeat what I perhaps had failed to understand.

Mrs. Phillips was a friend of Mrs. Kennedy, the organist at the Monumental Baptist Church, and learned from her that I could sing. She found a place for me on

(76)

I Leave the Farm

the eighth-grade Commencement program, and when her brother, Professor Calhoun, returned from Oberlin and gave a concert in our church, she persuaded Mrs. Kennedy to give me a solo part in an anthem which the choir sang on that occasion. Mr. Calhoun heard me sing my small solo and invited me to go for a walk with him after the concert. He offered to coach me, and presently I became his pupil. Another miracle had come to pass!

I took two lessons a week, for which I paid fifty cents a lesson. Ma was inclined to think that I was wasting my money. She thought it was impossible for Negroes to make a profession out of singing, except perhaps in minstrel shows and amongst low company. She wanted me to work at my books so that I might be a preacher. I respected her judgment, which after all only corresponded with the best judgment of most of the world at that time, and I tried to keep my mind on my studies. I thought to sit lightly to my singing, yet I had not been studying with Calhoun for more than two or three months before I had privately resolved to make a career of my music. I set my heart on going to the Oberlin Conservatory, where my teacher had studied.

Until I met Professor Calhoun I had heard very little white folks' music, apart from some Victorian anthems which we sang in church, and perhaps he did not teach me much pure music himself. Still, I owe to him my first hearing of great voices in classical songs and traditional arias; for if he let me sing pieces like "I Love You Truly," "The End of a Perfect Day," and "Forgotten," he also made it possible for me to hear distinguished music sung by Caruso, Scotti and Melba through the horn of a phonograph. My dormant senses were awakened by Caruso's matchless tones and taught to lend themselves to musical enchantment.

After perhaps a year with Mr. Calhoun, I was invited to go with him to the house of Mr. William Stone, the editor of the *Chattanooga Times*. A dinner party was in progress when we arrived, and Calhoun left me to sit out the early evening alone in the hall, until the guests had departed and the family were ready to hear me. The songs I had prepared were sufficiently banal — "The Lost Chord," I think, and "Oh, Happy Day." Mr. Stone asked me if I could sing "*Il Bacio*," a florid waltz by the Piedmontese composer, Luigi Arditi. I happened to know that romantic composition, a work in which both passion and notation reach D above high C, and performed it to the best of my ability.

Then Mr. Stone introduced me to that wonder of the age, the phonograph, and with it, to the finished art of singing. Indeed, it was then I received my first intimation that singing is an art. On my way home I mentally went over the songs of Caruso again and again, arias

(78)

from the operas of Verdi, Donizetti, and Puccini. That night I determined to become an artist myself. Twenty years later a Spanish critic spoke of me as the Negro Caruso.

As soon as I had a little repertoire of my own, Professor Calhoun invited me to appear with him at some of his concerts, and gave me useful experience in concert management as well. Management became a necessary part of my career for a long time, because as a Negro I could not find a manager at home until I had made a name for myself abroad.

One time Calhoun sent me down to Rome, a small Georgia city accessible to Chattanooga by means of a single daily train. He already had a booking there, but he wanted to be sure that the concert was being properly advertised. I went down a day early and found that the colored Baptists had done everything that was necessary to exploit our appearance. I had nothing to do but wait for the professor's arrival. The next day I went to the station to meet him. The train pulled in; he was not on it.

I paced up and down the streets of Rome until evening, dreading to break the news to the pastor of the church where we were supposed to sing and play. When I finally took courage and spoke to him, he told me that I must provide some kind of entertainment myself.

Angel Mo' and Her Son, Roland Hayes

I explained that I was not a concert performer. I could, I said diffidently, strum a kind of primitive accompaniment for my own simple songs . . . The minister bade me sing as many of them as I could remember, for as long a time as possible. He meant to see that his people got their money's worth. He introduced me to the congregation, most of which had assembled long before the appointed hour, and I sat down at the piano and began to improvise. Sounding a sustaining chord here and there, I sang all the songs I knew. I sang for over an hour. The audience wanted more. I was reduced to sheer invention.

I invented a story about a preacher and a bear. First I made up the story and then I sang it. It was about a preacher who went out hunting on a Sunday morning. He met a bear and took to a 'simmon tree. The bear sat looking at him hungrily. The preacher begged piteously to be allowed to come down. He had to get back to church in time for meeting. But the bear sat still. It was the judgment of God.

I think I had picked up the outline of the story at a minstrel show in Chattanooga. It was a classic, in its way, and I wish I could sing it now. I can remember only a scrap of the tune. I sang until I was tired out and my voice was husky. At last the audience filed out, leaving a trickle of nickels and dimes in a basin at the door. The B.Y.P.U. got half of the proceeds and I

I Leave the Farm

got the other, a good fifteen dollars, three days' wages for an evening's work. Perhaps, thought I, there is fortune as well as fame in the art of singing.

III

In the summer of 1905 I gave up my job — I had returned to work after my year in the fifth grade — and asked Ma for my share of the family savings. I wanted to go away and study music. She gave me fifty dollars from my own earnings, and although she did not exactly give me her blessing — indeed, she hoped that I would change my mind before the money was gone — she let me go out to find my way alone. I started for Nashville, expecting to go on in the fall to Oberlin. On the day of my arrival, Tom Key, a medical student who went with one of my cousins, took me for a walk through the campus of Fisk University, whose lawns and lanes were dominated by the cupolas and dormers of a shining palace, where for four years I was to make what seemed to me to be a prince's progress.

During the first decade of the history of Fisk, immediately after the War Between the States, the various schools were housed in the battered frame buildings of a military hospital, and the first teachers were soldiers who remained behind when the Northern army went home. In his introduction to a book called *The Singing*

Angel Mo' and Her Son, Roland Hayes

Campaign for Ten Thousand Pounds, a description of the travels of the Fisk Jubilee Singers in Great Britain, the Reverend E. M. Cravath traces the transition from hospital and morgue to seat of learning: to "fountain of life and light and inspiration." Teachers occupied the officers' quarters; sick-wards, left empty by the evacuation of wounded soldiers, became schoolrooms; and the old morgue was stored with supplies to feed and clothe the first scholars of my race.

Four graduates of the original high-school department formed the first college class in 1871, and in the same year a choir was sent out on tour to raise money for a new campus with ampler buildings. The Jubilee Singers sang two seasons of concerts in the United States and a season in Great Britain. They made nearly a hundred thousand dollars, and built Jubilee Hall in the midst of a new twenty-five-acre campus. I had not thought that so splendid a structure existed this side of the moon.

I was anxious to give some concerts during my visit to Nashville. I had a program for a full evening of music, with the *"Erlkönig"* for a sure-fire climax, and I hoped to earn some money for my tuition at Oberlin. Tom Key introduced me to colored clergymen who invited me to go shares on recitals in their churches. I sang my program many times, but out of my "share"

I Leave the Farm

of the customary silver offerings I had to pay so many
expenses that by the end of the summer, although I had
made a little reputation for myself, I had spent all of
my earnings as well as all of the money Ma gave me.
I made inquiries about entering Fisk, only to be reminded how slight my resources were. My fifth-grade
education hardly made me a suitable candidate for college, and besides, I could not pay the tuition.

A kind lady, Miss Stubbs, a public-school teacher,
offered to take me out to the campus to meet Miss
Robinson, the director of the department of music.
When we reached her office in Jubilee Hall, Miss Robin-
son was on her way out to keep an urgent engagement.
A tall woman with a thin, elongated face and unsmiling, puritanical expression, she was polite but not
especially cordial. She begged to be excused. Persistent
Miss Stubbs persuaded her to give me one minute. Miss
Robinson led us to a reception room, where she asked
me about my education and probed into my private
economy. Miss Stubbs came breathlessly to my rescue.
She asked Miss Robinson to let me sing, first of all.
I had two ragged sheets of music in my pocket, "Beyond the Gates of Paradise," and "Forgotten." I sang
from them, as I had been taught, with expression.
Nothing in Miss Robinson's countenance suggested that
my singing sounded good in her ears.

Angel Mo' and Her Son, Roland Hayes

"Wherever did you learn such sentimental rubbish?" she said.

My heart went down into my boots. And as though she were punishing me for causing her to miss her appointment, Miss Robinson kept me by her for an hour to tell me it was impossible to receive me into the school. Miss Stubbs pleaded with her to speak about me to Dr. Merrill, the President. Accordingly, I received permission to come back the following day. But Miss Robinson's voice held out no promise. I went away feeling that my musical taste was contemptible.

I was low in my mind and the next day seemed a long way off. I returned to my hired attic room and prayed. I wrestled with God, like Jacob. I did not leave my room until I returned alone to Jubilee Hall twenty-four hours later.

Miss Robinson was standing on the front stairway when I approached that inhospitable building whose magnificence now failed to cheer me. Her face and her voice were as economical of expression as her reading of music. She handed me a slip of paper and sent me off to the President's office. I went trembling into that great man's presence and was terrified to see a spectacled individual with a big Roman nose and heavy, overhanging eyebrows.

I Leave the Farm

"The man is an eagle," I said to myself. "He is the American eagle himself."

I handed my slip of paper to a secretary. Presently the eagle turned his gaze upon me. After quite a long time he shot questions at me, without stopping to listen to my answers. Who was I? What was my name? Where did I live? Why had I come to Fisk? Why did I come without money? How did I mean to get on? How did he know whether I was fit to enter the school? When he had finished frightening me, he posted me off to the head of the academic department for impromptu examination.

I took my tests on the spot, orally: in arithmetic, geography, and reading. I also recited a poem. Then I was sent back to Dr. Merrill with a note which said that I was at best a fifth-grader. He read the note aloud, giving me ample time to ponder it. Then, quite unexpectedly, his face broke up, its severity lost in deep, kind lines. He told me he had got me a job as furnace boy and waiter in a judge's home, and admitted me into the lower school on probation.

Before night I was installed in a room over a stable. My head reeled with instructions about tending furnace and cutting grass and serving table. Molly, the cook, had shown me how to lay silver and exchange heirloom

(*85*)

china plates. With board and room secure, and a dollar a week for my pocket, I began my college life.

IV

I worked for two years for Mr. and Mrs. Lyon Childress and old Judge Childress in their fine house in the aristocratic West End of Nashville, walking every morning across the city to my classes. Mr. Childress was a young lawyer, a distinguished and sleepy-looking man with light hair and a fair complexion. He had only lately married a tall, rather heavy woman, who had a dark, Spanish look about her. She appeared to be indolent, too, but actually she had plenty of energy when some particular cause evoked it. She used to call me "her boy Roland," and when I went back to Nashville to sing in 1923, she turned the city upside down to get people out to hear me.

During my third year at Fisk I worked on the campus as butler to Professor Warren G. Waterman, a Yankee chemist, an excessively tall man with black hair, sunburned skin, and a consumptive stoop. His wife was a German woman, short and thick of stature, and blonde and jolly — although entirely unsentimental. She was a fine musician, and both of them were good livers.

Professor Waterman had a collection of phonograph records of which he was extremely careful. One cold winter morning, when I was having trouble with the furnace, I sang at it — instead of swearing — at the top of my voice. Professor Waterman rushed downstairs in a rage, as he told me years later, expecting to catch me playing the phonograph. At the time, I was unable to understand why it was that he suddenly began to invite me to sit in the living room and listen to his records; but as it happened, his self-imposed penance, whilst it eased the Professor's conscientious mind, had the effect of considerably augmenting my musical education.

During the fourth and last year of my life at the University I lived in the men's dormitory, Livingston Hall, where, in return for being soloist at all sorts of academic functions, I received — or so I supposed at the time — free tuition, board, and lodging. Thus I had a little more leisure than I had been accustomed to, time enough indeed to have a girl of my own — although I was able to see precious little of her.

It is old Southern doctrine that any unobserved Negro, man or boy, will commit rape at the slightest opportunity. It was therefore a rule at Fisk that students should be under constant surveillance. There was a definite schedule of hours for calling on girls who lived in the women's dormitory. A boy was expected to ask permission to make an engagement with his girl, and when he called to keep it, he was met by a chaperon who sat in plain sight throughout the evening. Girls were only rarely permitted to go out after dark, and then they went in squads, led by lady sergeant-majors.

A rhetorical at the chapel was the occasion of my first important date with Mattie, who was about the most attractive girl that I had ever met. Not since the days when we used to pair off after choir practice at the Monumental Baptist Church had I known such African beauty. She carried herself proudly, and her face was like a dusky melon. I called for her at Jubilee Hall, along with all the other young men who lived in my dormitory, and presented myself to the preceptress. I made a correct bow to Mattie and accompanied her in a decorous procession down a brightly lighted avenue to the church. We sat together at the rhetorical, and when the program was over we returned in company to Jubilee Hall. That was about as much of each other's society as Fisk boys and girls were allowed to have at one time. Since we were not permitted to stop and pass the time of day together on the campus, I never really saw Mattie alone. Presently she married a more accessible boy of her own set in Rome.

At the end of my fourth year, after the terminal examinations and while I was in the midst of rehearsals with the Jubilee Singers, Miss Robinson sent for me.

I Leave the Farm

She asked me to return all the music I had borrowed from the library. I said, "Yes, ma'am," and turned to leave. Miss Robinson stopped me. She hoped I understood that I was being dismissed from the University. I tried to ask questions, but she was adamant in her refusal to discuss the circumstances with me.

Overwhelmed with grief and disappointment, I went to see Professor Waterman and told him of the shock I had received. He made inquiries and discovered, first of all, that Miss Robinson had personally undertaken to find the means to pay my tuition and support me at Fisk all those years. She had exacted money for me from her friends. It was suggested to me that in spending so much time with the Jubilee Singers, I had perhaps failed to do justice to my work in the department of music, which traditionally had nothing to do with the celebrated chorus; but I was never able to find out whether that was the case. Professor Waterman advised me to be contented with what, in four years, I had already got out of my studies there, and go on to something else. After discovering that I had not actually been supporting myself, as I had thought, I had no alternative to withdrawing as sensibly as I could.

In a final effort to reinstate myself, I searched my conscience and went to the President. I said I would apologize if my fault were made clear to me. Perhaps I was not altogether disingenuous, because I was angry as well as hurt. The President quite properly refused to act over Miss Robinson's head. As gently as possible he reaffirmed my expulsion.

Ex-student as I was, I was invited by the director of the Jubilee Singers to stay on and take my part in the Commencement rhetorical. When my solo was announced, Miss Robinson, ever relentless in the promulgation of her principles, ostentatiously left the chapel. I was sick at heart; but afterwards, when I was able to think of her without agitation, I had to admit that she had always been as severe with herself as she was with her pupils and colleagues. Quick, dry and peppery of speech, she walked stiffly and yielded nothing to impulse. No ornament ever adorned her person, her conversation, or her manners. She was an austere devotee of pure music. "The composer's sentiment is written into his music," she would say, "and it is a vulgarity in the singer to add to the sentiment written into the notes." Perhaps she thought the Jubilee standard was not so refined.

I was happy when Miss Robinson was reconciled to me, some years later, because I was so much in her debt for what she had done for me, a hardly literate, an untrained and impoverished boy. She had given me a sound musical foundation and had seen to it that I learned the rudiments of history, rhetoric, and literature as well. Professor Calhoun had taught me some Schubert, note for note, coaching me on the vocal line until I could sing it without a sustaining accompaniment; but before I became Miss Robinson's pupil, I had only a vague knowledge of reading and notation. First of all, I learned to read notes at the piano, and my taste for classical music was gradually developed by singing the great oratorios: the "Saint Paul" and "Elijah" of Mendelssohn; Cardinal Newman's "Dream of Gerontius," set to music by Sir Edward Elgar; Haydn's "Seven Last Words," and the *Christus am Ölberge* of Beethoven.

I may say for myself that when I left Nashville, I was not afraid of any work that might lie ahead of me. I was used to hard work and actually took comfort in it. My mother used to quote the Gospel text, "If thine eye be single, thy whole body shall be full of light." She had brought us up to be single-eyed, to concentrate on a task and finish it without diversion. I went to work early, to help repair our desperate poverty, and early learned to express my whole nature in necessary motion, so to speak. But I could not help wondering, as I sadly said farewell to Fisk, how in the world I should get on with my voice.

Professor Waterman advised me to go to Louisville, where there was a choral society under the direction of a trustee of the University. I got a job at the Pendennis Club and joined a new quartet. One of the members of the club introduced me to an opera director who considered ways and means of turning me into a white man, so that he could take me into a company which he had brought to Louisville for a fortnight's run. Nothing came of that project, but a local theatrical manager found a way to put my disembodied voice to use. He stood me inoffensively behind a moving-picture screen to sing arias illustrating silent operatic "shorts."

Just before the expiration of the contract for my ghostly services, which had netted me forty dollars a week, the President of Fisk offered me the post of leading tenor with the Jubilee Singers, who were rehearsing for a summer conference to be called "The World in Boston." I signed up for fifty dollars a month and expenses, because I was willing to go to Boston at any price. A gentleman from that city had told me that if Nashville was the Athens of the South, Boston was truly the Athens of America. I returned to Nashville in time for Commencement, exactly a year after my expulsion, and I sang at the graduation rhetorical. Miss Robinson stayed away from chapel altogether on that occasion; she still found my presence on the campus insupportable. I thought I had done very well by myself that year in Louisville. I had become a man in years as well as in stature. But this reminder of my failure to meet with Miss Robinson's approval gave me a fresh set of misgivings. I became fearful lest I should lose the initiative which had so far sustained me.

Over the generations we Negroes have lost our self-direction. We were brought willy-nilly to this country and learned to eat the bread of masters whom we did not freely serve. After the Surrender we received physical and political freedom, but our minds and souls were still enslaved. I had lived for a few years in Nashville in the company of men and women who were dedicated to the life of the mind, and I came to desire that order of self-liberation more than anything else. I wanted to belong to that small group of Negroes who were showing our race the way towards the only real freedom, the freedom to produce and to create. I hoped for strength to go straight after those objects when I reached the North.

Before my trip to Boston I went to Chattanooga to take leave of my mother. My brother Robert had married and moved to Los Angeles, Baby Jesse had become a messboy with the fleet, and Ma was living alone. She took in washing and still milked her own cow. I found her heating kettles of water over coals she had picked up in the railroad yards. I told her that I was going to look for a job in Boston before the Jubilee Singers came home. I promised her that I would come and fetch her, and make a home for her up there. But

Angel Mo' and Her Son, Roland Hayes

Mother was not yet convinced that I could make a career for myself as a singer. She recited all the familiar objections. Colored people, she said, could not hope to understand white folks' songs, and white folks would not listen to serious music coming out of Negro mouths.

It was with bitter sorrow that at length I said farewell to my mother. I had wanted so much to go away with her blessing. A lonely time lay ahead of us both. I knew I should be desolate; and how bereft Ma was I discovered, years later, in a letter she wrote to Robert after her first Christmas alone.

BRANTIE HAYES, DEAR SON [she said],

Here is another letter. I know you have not answered my last letter, but I thought I would write anyway and let you hear from me, whether you want to or not. This leaves me as common, hope this will find you both the same. I think everybody was made glad on Christmas day, both rich and poor, according to what the paper says, but I have not enjoyed the Christmas much.

She had been sitting up night after night with a sick nephew, Uncle Wiltsie's son. He had been so "low" that she was sure he was going to die. All tired out, so tired she "can't harly write," she commits her children to the Lord's watchful care. God alone companioned her solitude.

CHAPTER FOUR

I Go to Boston

MY LIFE has fallen into sharply separated epochs, and when I look back upon the events which compose them — and especially upon the concluding episodes of each — I find the intervals so attenuated that I feel as though I had died often, and often come to life again.

I died first to the farm and then to core making. I suffered and was buried when Miss Robinson disowned me. I left my wonted self behind in Boston in 1920, the year I went to England, where a wholly different way of life was opened up before me. A nearly devastating break occurred at the abrupt conclusion to the rich decade which followed, when I saw my career beginning to disintegrate before my eyes, my fortune vanish, my expansive plans for the enrichment of Negro culture shrunk to the narrow compass of a Georgia farm.

Each of my personal epochs has been tied to its predecessor by the thin line of a single appetite. I wanted always to find new and ampler clothing for the frame of my voice. When I first dreamed of being a great artist, back in Chattanooga in 1904, how small and spare a frame my voice possessed, how scanty were my means to clothe it! The voice of Caruso pouring out of the horn of a primitive phonograph had seemed to me to come from some remote and inaccessible heaven where a kind of light shone, and where voices had achieved a rich substantiality; but of the techniques of approach to that musical paradise I was wholly ignorant.

For a time at Fisk I had lived in a Garden of Eden, albeit an abstemious and lonely Adam, waiting for some divine operation: such as the habilitation of my vocal chords. Expulsion from that Eden, before my purpose was accomplished, had come near to being the death of me; and it was not until I had overcome the baffling prevenience of poverty that I was able to plunder Boston on behalf of a voice which, in May 1911, was still nearly as naked as a jaybird. I was not afraid of poverty. I was a good workman and willing to work. I did not care if I had to work ten thousand days. Up North, I thought, if I were to lay out a penitential way of life, I should at length be clothed in mind and voice: for until my nakedness was covered I felt I could not walk upright again.

I have not the slightest idea what Boston looked like on the night of my arrival there, more than thirty years ago. I had only one thing on my mind, and that was to deliver, as quickly as possible, a letter from the Pendennis Club to a businessman named Mr. Henry H. Putnam, whom I had met in Louisville. By the time Mr. Putnam arrived at his office, on the morning after I reached Boston, I was standing at his door with the letter in my hand.

"How much money have you got?" he asked, after he had read it.

"I have a hundred dollars," I said.

"Where is it?" he inquired.

"I have it on me," I answered.

Mr. Putnam took me to the Five Cents Savings Bank and showed me how to deposit my money. He promised to ask some musicians to give me a hearing and sent me back to my job with the Jubilee Singers. I waited nervously to hear from him — eating what I was given to eat, sleeping where a bed had been provided, and walking the streets in search of work. I think I visited every hotel employment office from Copley Square to the gilded dome on Beacon Hill and down to the shabby environs of Boston Harbor.

At length Mr. Putnam's message came. He had arranged for me to sing to five teachers. I went first to Mr. Theodore Parker, whose system was to teach tonal quality by way of the violin. He listened to me in silence and I went as silently away. I sang then at the St. Botolph Club for Mr. Charles White, who taught at the New England Conservatory of Music. He was a little more encouraging. Next, I visited Mr. Arthur Foote, the organist and composer. Mr. Foote, a thin-faced man, keen of feature and spare of body, had made some charming songs from Irish poems, but he asked me for operatic arias. When I had sung what I knew, he showed me how to interpret them more faithfully — and passed me on to Mr. Benjamin Whelpley, another of the famous Boston teachers whose studios lined Newbury Street in those days.

At last I found my way to the Symphony Chambers, where I was received by Mr. Arthur J. Hubbard, a rough Yankee giant who both terrified and attracted me. He had been a pupil of Francesco Limperti in Milan, and in his day had made a career as an operatic basso profondo. He put me through my paces thoroughly and concluded that he was willing to take me as a pupil, provided I felt perfectly sure it was going to be worth my while to try to become a singer. He did not explain exactly what he meant, and I kept puzzling over the proviso until I went back to see Mr. Putnam.

"Two of the five gentlemen who have heard you are willing to teach you," he said, "and one of them is ready to give you a scholarship. But I want to warn you that every man-Jack of them believes it is quite impossible for a Negro to be accepted as a serious artist."

Eight years later, when I had sung all over the country in concerts I had managed myself, I asked a Boston manager if he would take over my bookings. I was confronted even then by the same hard, bleak wall of prejudice.

"Hayes," he said, "you know that I'm your friend. I want to advise you as sensibly as I can. In my opinion, you have got about as far as you can go in this country. The American public will never cotton to you."

I can say truly that never in my whole life have I wished I were a white man; but I confess that there were times, long ago, when it seemed difficult to be a Negro in a white world. In the South, I had been carefully taught my "place," and I did not suppose that in the North my place would be, in the beginning, less restricted than at home: but I had somehow hoped that I would not so frequently be reminded of it. My mother had often quoted the verse, "The way of transgressors is hard," but it sometimes seemed unjust, when I was trying with all my heart to be prudent, that my soul, like the transgressor's, had so often to eat violence. I was determined, however, not to be permanently put down.

I liked Mr. Hubbard, for all his gruffness, and wanted

to study with him. It was agreed that I should begin in the autumn to take lessons in the evening at his house in Dorchester: at his house, so that I should not embarrass him by appearing in his studio amongst his white pupils, many of whom were Southern boys and girls; and in the evening, so that I could support myself by working in the daytime. I undertook to pay five dollars a lesson.

After the final concert of The World in Boston, the director ordered the choir to prepare to return to Nashville. I had then to tell him that I was going to stay in Boston. He was indignant.

"What would your mother say?" he asked.

"I have told my mother."

"You'll starve," he said.

"No," said I. "I have a job at the Brunswick Hotel on Boylston Street."

"But suppose the job doesn't last?"

"I have a hundred dollars in the bank," I said. He gave me up.

After a month of wrestling brass spittoons — the bell-boys called them puppies — I joined two of my college friends in Atlantic City, where we all went to work as waiters in a restaurant on the Million Dollar Pier. One night, near the end of the summer, I ceremoniously presented a broiled and garnished steak for the approval of a man who had brought five or six guests in to dinner. The gentleman, a little the worse for drink, seemed to take an instant dislike to both the steak and me.

"Take that steak back to the unprintable kitchen, you nigger son-of-a-bitch," he shouted.

I plopped the platter down on a serving table and took up a carving knife. I think my manner must have suggested that I was getting ready to carve the customer instead of the steak, for the headwaiter and his lieutenants hustled me speedily into the kitchen. The headwaiter took my part, when the story was repeated to the boss, and I was not fired; but after a few days my companions and I formed a quartet, with another boy named O'Hara, so we gave up our jobs to go out on the town.

In the fall, I got a temporary job distributing campaign cards for the Republican Club of Boston. One of the members, an officer of the John Hancock Company, asked me one day what I intended to do for a living after election. I told him that I was looking for a job that would enable me to bring my mother to Boston.

"You can go tomorrow and fetch her," he said. "Come back a week from next Monday and you can go to work for us. We will pay you seven dollars a week."

Angel Mo' and Her Son, Roland Hayes

Mr. Hubbard, with whom I had so far taken only a lesson or two, lent me seventy-five dollars and I went to Chattanooga to get Ma. We sold the old cow for what she would bring and bought a large packing case. We stuffed the box full of Ma's household possessions: feather ticking, sheets and pillow slips, quilts and blankets, towels and tablecloths, flatirons, pots and pans and china dishes; and checked it on our railway tickets. Ma was very quiet all the way to Boston.

Some friends invited us to stay with them in Roxbury until we could find rooms of our own. Ma was restless because she could find nothing to do in their immaculate house. Misery set in, and Ma was sure that she could get well again only in her own home. We moved our few possessions into an unfurnished apartment in Westminster Street, and Ma's misery departed. A scrubbing brush in her hand and good boards under her knees were medicine enough.

I made a bed for my mother out of the packing-case lumber, and two little stools for the hearth. Ma disappeared from the house for a few minutes, after I had shown her the benches, and came back with an armful of wood which she had salvaged from the street. She made a bright fire in the fireplace and we drew up our stools and sat down. Out of the corner of my eye I watched my mother's face, with the firelight full upon it. I have never seen a more contented expression on the face of any human being. We had no stove, no table, no cupboard, but we had each other. We had founded a home in a strange city.

I paid four dollars a week for the apartment and sixty cents for carfare. That left us with two dollars and forty cents a week for food and fuel. I had to begin right away to earn money by singing, in order to pay for my lessons. Mr. Hubbard let me go to his studio, after a time, to take my turn at auditions given by choir directors. Sometimes he even introduced me as his star pupil, but usually the white folks only shook their heads.

Just before Easter, the year after I settled in Boston, I had somehow managed to get an engagement to sing in a church in New Hampshire. It was canceled, almost at the last moment, on account of scarlet fever, and Mr. Hubbard recommended me to another out-of-town church. I happened to be in his studio when somebody telephoned to say that the music committee had decided not to take me. I could see Mr. Hubbard bristle. He clutched the receiver with a strangle hold and roared into the mouthpiece.

"You tell your church people verbatim," he thundered, "that they may be followers of the meek and lowly Jesus, but at a hell of a long ways off."

Angel Mo' and Her Son, Roland Hayes

The message was straightway delivered, the committee engaged me, and until I went to England in 1920 I was the Easter soloist at that church every year.

The stringency of our household economy was considerably relaxed when Miss Annie Cleaveland Bridgman began to take an interest in me. Miss Bridgman was for thirty years the secretary of the New England office of the American Missionary Association in Boston, and worked all her life for the advancement of my people. She recommended me to a Baptist church in Newton Center, where for a time I earned five dollars a Sunday, and under her patronage I soon had a profitable engagement every week. A year before she died in Northampton, where she lived after her retirement, I gave a concert at Smith College, and I called on her then to thank her once more for all she had done for my mother and me.

By the time I had paid off my debt to Mr. Hubbard, my mother was ready to make a visit to her family and friends in Chattanooga. She felt strange in the North and longed for a glimpse of home. I bought her a round-trip ticket, some percale dresses and a worsted coat, and saw her off for the South. Within ten days she wrote that she was coming back to Boston. I had taken a better apartment, to surprise her, and I needed a few more days to furnish it. I therefore urged her to stay out the month, as she had planned, but I had hardly posted my letter before she turned up.

"I didn't like it down there, son," she said. "Folks carry on too much foolishness."

"That is what you used to say about folks in Boston," I protested.

"Ain't so much foolishness round here as dey is in Chattanooga," she said. "Ev'ything is all different down there now."

In Boston, Ma no longer dipped snuff, in deference to Northern prejudice, and I fancied, for one thing, that she hated to see her old friends still taking it, down there in the South. Although I had persuaded her, quite against her current impulse, not to sell the farm in Curryville, she never spoke again, when we were traveling in a southerly direction, of going "home."

Ma made a religious habit of plain living. She almost never bought anything for herself, and only rarely allowed me to give her some small luxury. When I brought presents home she would show pleasure in my thought of her, but lest she should encourage me in prodigality, she would invariably say, "Of course I don't really need this, son. I have everything I want. I came here to help you, not to spend you out."

When Ma came back from Chattanooga I was half fearful of showing her around our new apartment, but she was so glad to be back that she did not scold me for extravagance.

"Lawsy, son, here's a bed, here's a real bed of my own," she exclaimed. And she loved a wicker rocking chair which I had covered with dark-green paint and tufted in some light-green stuff. She used to pin her pocketbook to a flowered and beribboned headrest which I had suspended from the top of the chair — a gesture of appropriation which always seemed to me to be quaint and touching, considering that Mother was generally so detached from her physical possessions.

II

In 1914 there came to Boston the secretary of Dr. Booker Taliaferro Washington, a great hero to Americans of my race, to find a tenor who could sing duets with the Negro composer and baritone singer, Harry T. Burleigh, on one of Dr. Washington's lecture tours. I was pleased when he chose me to travel in that distinguished company. I had not yet met Dr. Washington, but I had long since been familiar with the story of Harry Burleigh's performance of "Swing Low, Sweet Chariot" for Anton Dvořák, the Czech composer, back in the 1890's. The melody of that spiritual appears, slightly disguised, as the second theme of the first movement of the "New World Symphony." With Dvořák's encouragement, Burleigh had jotted down traditional musical settings for some of our Afro-American songs. Traveling about with him, I felt close to the inspired sources of our native music.

Dr. Washington's lectures expounded a single theme: the necessity and the dignity of agricultural and industrial education. He felt that the greatest good to the nation, as well as to the Negro race, would come out of the elevation of the greatest number of people; and the greatest number of people in any race and country work with their hands.

Not all of the Negro intellectuals of our time have embraced the realistic doctrines of Booker T. Washington — although his teaching has radically modified the curricula of thousands of schools, for white children and Negro children alike. The Du Bois theory of education which begins, by contrast, not at the bottom but at the top, has appealed to most aspirants to professional careers, the sons and daughters of wealthier Negroes. I myself was quite won over, in 1914, by Dr. Washington's democratic realism, and I have always wanted to make of my farm in Georgia a working illustration of his noble teaching: a place where young artists may begin life close to the soil. Some of us must advance beyond the rudiments, as Du Bois believes and teaches; but our racial culture ought to rest on the solid foundation of skill in factory and field. I may be old-fashioned, but I like to think that I am a better singer for having learned to plow a straight furrow when I was a boy in the Flatwoods.

One night after a lecture in the Town Hall in Attleboro, Dr. Washington proposed that we walk part of the way to Boston over a dusty back-country road. At every railroad crossing we learned that we had missed the last train to the city. We had walked many a mile, and Dr. Washington was limping, when we tottered into the outskirts of Quincy, where we hoped at last to pick up a haul.

"Take my arm, Dr. Washington," said Harry Burleigh. "I guess this is one time when you've had enough of the soil."

News of my public appearance with such great men as Booker T. Washington and Harry Burleigh filtered back to Nashville. In a letter of congratulation, my estranged teacher, Miss Robinson, suggested that it was time for us to bury the hatchet. I replied that I should be glad if she would bury hers. For myself, I said, I had never carried one. This I endeavored to prove by going down to Fisk University to sing "Elijah," with Burleigh in the baritone lead and me in the narrative part. We became good friends again, Miss Robinson and I, and when she died she left me all of her teaching notes. I took them to Paris, where I was living then, and I hope I may live to see the day when I can bring them home.

On my visit to Nashville I discovered that my Cousin Helen Alzada Mann had grown up to be an attractive young woman, still not quite out of her teens. She was only about six years old when my mother and brothers and I had moved up from the farm to the city, whereas I had been nearly a man, going on fourteen. As far as I was concerned, Alzada was then only a little giggling girl, although I could not help but notice how pretty she was. From 1907 to 1911, when she was in high school, I seldom saw her, and then for three years I never laid eyes on her at all.

A day or two before the concert I called on her at the normal school which she had come to Nashville to attend. I was very proud to have such a charming cousin. She was beautifully educated — all of the women of her generation in the family have gone to college — and had poise and sparkle, together with a good measure of inherited mother-wit. She treated me with the most flattering respect, introducing me to her teachers with little speeches that were calculated to hint at the nature of my reputation, and thus modestly, perhaps, to enhance her own. I was "Buddie" to Alzada, and now that I was so nearly a stranger in my old homeland, Alzada

was "family" to me. When I went back to Fisk the
next year, as I did every year until I went abroad to
live, Alzada was no longer there — she had finished
her training course — and I missed her.

In the summer of 1915 I toured the Pennsylvania
Chautauqua Circuit with William Lawrence and William Richardson. Lawrence, who afterwards accompanied me for a number of years in Europe, was somewhat younger than I, a good-looking, copper-colored
youth with not a little elegance of dress and deportment.
We called ourselves the Hayes Trio and collected a
hundred and seventy-five dollars a week. Having begun
to think of ourselves as artists, we tried to look like
artists. We wore stiff collars and flowing black ties, one-
button black jackets, white-flannel trousers, and white-
buckskin shoes. We sang Beethoven, Schubert, Rubin-
stein, and the obscure Venetian, Polani. If we were
unduly solemn, the two Williams and I, it was because
we all felt that we had important work to do and a
long way to go.

I am embarrassed to recall that in my preoccupation
with the European composers, and with learning French
and German, I had become neglectful of Afro-American music. I did not sing a single spiritual at my Jordan
Hall concert in Boston the following winter. I suppose
I was unconsciously putting myself into competition

with white singers, whose spotlight I wanted to share.
I had not yet received the revelation which was presently to give my ambition its native direction. I had set
out to become an artist, but I had still to learn that I
must approach art personally; I had still to be taught
that I, Roland Hayes, a Negro, had first to measure my
racial inheritance and then to put it to use. It remained
for me to learn, humbly at first, and then with mounting
confidence, that my way to artistry was a Negro way.

No professional manager would sponsor my first important concert in Boston, and I lacked the experience
to make it a financial success by myself. The critics,
and especially Philip Hale, the arbiter of Athenian taste
at that time, encouraged me to believe that I had made
an artistic success, but I lost two hundred dollars of
hard-earned savings. To accumulate capital for another
venture, I went on a tour of Negro churches in a dozen
Southern cities, and two years later, in 1917, against the
advice of my teacher and most of my friends, I announced a concert in Symphony Hall.

Unable to interest an established management in my
project, I engaged a secretary who helped me to compile
a mailing list of three thousand people. I sold eight hundred dollars' worth of tickets in that way, and had so
many patrons and patronesses that it cost me a fortune
to print their names in the program.

Angel Mo' and Her Son, Roland Hayes

I do not mean to suggest that the public was unanimously responsive. The wife of the then Governor of the Commonwealth wrote to say, in effect, "I cannot let my name be attached to an enterprise which is bound to be a failure before it begins." I read that letter over and over again to see if it meant something not so cruelly on the surface, but I could find no hidden message to console me. And again, when I put paid advertisements in the papers, on the recommendation of Philip Hale, there was a storm of protests from the general public. I hurried to the booking offices in Symphony Hall and paid forthwith the rental charge of four hundred dollars. I patted the pocket where I had deposited the receipt for my money and reflected that nothing now could stop me from doing as I pleased.

Even my Negro friends, many of them, thought the concert would be a calamity. Nevertheless, along with white friends, fellow employees who had heard me singing in the corridors of the John Hancock Building, they bought box-office tickets by the hundred, and filled the hall — floor, balcony, and stage — to overflowing. Seven hundred people, so it was said, were turned away. In the artists' room before the concert I was nearly out of my mind with fatigue and excitement, but I sang through my program without faltering: three groups of songs of the classical and romantic composers

(*112*)

I Go to Boston

and a final group of spirituals. I sang *"Du bist die Ruh"* and other songs of Schubert, and works of Mozart and Tchaikovsky. There was no Bach in my repertoire as yet, and although I was studying French with Mme. Emelie Alexandra Marius, the first American woman to be elected to the French Academy, I was not yet ready with Debussy and Duparc.

Many of my special friends came to hear me, amongst them General and Mrs. Russell, whose house is now my Brookline home. The Russells had kept a secret station on the "Underground Railroad" before the War Between the States, and their daughter, Miss Mary Russell, a charter member of the Boston Symphony Society, had introduced me to the music of Tchaikovsky. As a compliment to her I sang some of her favorite songs that night.

My mother came to the concert and was proud of me. She walked through the colored community with her head high after that.

III

Early in 1918, I started out on a cross-country tour which I managed myself. I got out a prospectus which showed me in a belted and fur-lined overcoat and a pair of laced shoes with cream-colored tops. I announced myself as "Roland W. Hayes, Celebrated Ne-

gro Tenor"; quoted seven newspaper articles, including
one in which a *New York Tribune* reporter compared
me to the great French singer Clément; and gave notice
to churches and Negro fraternities that I was accept-
ing engagements for recitals and concerts, opera and
oratorios.

Lawrence Brown, who later became Paul Robeson's
accompanist, made that tour with me, and so did my
mother. Brown, who had come to Boston in 1917, from
Charleston, South Carolina, was on good terms with her.
She liked him because he was a good church boy, and
she often did his washing for nothing. He was a fine
figure of a young man, rather bigger than I, and with
brown curly hair and nice features.

We left Washington for the West in the midst of
a historical blizzard. Our train broke down in the
mountains of West Virginia, and for hours upon end
we were stalled in snowdrifts, suffering from cold and
hunger. Ma disappeared — head, feet, and body — under
a warm blanket from which she emerged only once,
and that was for the purpose of addressing a fellow
traveler who was complaining loud and bitterly.

"Put yo' haid under a blanket, like me, and make yo'
own heat," she said. That shut him up.

I sang in Chattanooga and afterwards in Nashville,
where I had the pleasure of introducing my mother to

I Go to Boston

Miss Robinson; and from there we went to St. Louis, to visit Poro College — a clinical establishment in which a group of ambitious young ladies was being instructed in the use and distribution of cosmetics. The proprietress had accumulated quite a comfortable fortune from ointments which make kinky hair straight. She had few competitors in her business, for the reason that the white unguentaries were busy compounding preparations to make straight hair kinky. Ma walked about amongst the laboratories and classrooms quoting Ecclesiastes on the subject of vanity.

I had taken my mother with me because I thought she would enjoy one more glimpse of the Flatwoods. Occasional letters from Curryville and Chattanooga used to make me nostalgic for the South, and I thought Ma might have been more homesick than she was willing to admit. There was a kind of pathetic formulism in some of those letters from our relatives. I feel the pathos still, as I read them again after all these years. I have seen translations of letters written by simple people in the Mediterranean countries two thousand years ago, and the formulas of hail and farewell contained in them remind me of others written to my mother by her Cousin Obey Mann — we called her Cousin Obie — who used to collect rent for Ma's farm in Curryville.

"Yore letter found us well and also leaves us all the

same. I hope that you are well, as your letter left you well." Such phrases as those are traditional amongst us. The forms are practically Hellenistic; but if they may be thought to suggest the secular correspondence of antiquity, so do Cousin Obie's benedictions recall the early Christian writers: "I'm still trying to live closter and closter to the Lord, for he is our dearest friend. He is above all. So good-bye, continue in the Faith, until death."

Ma enjoyed our visit with Aunt Harriet Cross and Cousin Obie, but I was disappointed when the rest of our excursion failed to give her all the pleasure I had planned. It seemed to her to be a worldly junket, once we had embarked upon it. She refused to go to parties which were arranged for us, and disapproved of my going to them alone. In Denver, where we stopped on the way to the Coast, Ma threatened to take the train to Los Angeles, where my brother Robert was living, because I insisted upon going to an entertainment after my concert. I tried to explain that I was sometimes obliged to meet my public. On that particular occasion, in fact, it was hoped that my appearance at a ball would help the management make up my not inconsiderable fee of two hundred and seventy-five dollars. I went to the party, promising to come home early, but when I returned I heard that my mother had left. I rushed to the railway station and found her trying to negotiate for a ticket to California.

"Why do you make it so difficult for me, Mother?" I asked. "If I am doing nothing morally wrong, you must trust me to do the best I can."

But nothing I could say would persuade her to go back to the house from which she had so unceremoniously departed. I went back to gather up our luggage and returned to the station, where we sat up all night in a chilly waiting room. Ma looked as pleased as if she had snatched me from the embrace of Satan himself. She grew neither weary nor cold in well-doing.

I received in Los Angeles a few days later a letter complimenting me upon my diction. Ma was better disposed toward me after that, for she had been trying to teach me how nearly sense is related to sound. One time, only a few weeks before the tour, she was out in her kitchen ironing while I was practising a song in the front room of our apartment. She called out, "What was that you said, Roland?"

"I'm just singing, Mother," I replied.

"But what did you *say?*" she insisted.

"But, Mother, I tell you I'm only singing," I said.

"Well," said she, "if you are singing words, I don't understand them. When you sing, I think you ought to say the words so that everybody can hear and understand." After that I tried not to mumble my words.

My correspondent also said that my voice reminded her of a "rich purplish red," and from that comment I got a really creative idea: an idea which, after considerable enlargement on my next visit to California, has borne fruit — or so I believe — throughout my career. In 1918 I had not yet given over trying to sing like a white man. It had not yet come to me, in so many words, that even the voice I was born with was colored. I began to listen more closely to white singers, and to my amazement I discovered that their voices were as white as their skins. A little later, Hulda Hervin Newhouse said of my voice, in one of her poems, that it was "colored like old mellowed wine," and I thought of the "rich purplish red" of Burgundy. It was an exciting idea, although I cannot say that I turned it over as inquisitively then as I did later.

It was early summer when my mother and I crossed the country on our way back to Boston. I shall always remember that part of our journey because I was relaxed and happy. I filled my notebook with poems in which I recorded my observations of the beautiful green countryside in such lines as these: —

> The grasses are green on field and hill,
>   Their petals are wet with dew,
> And in an early morning hour
>   The sun comes streaming through.

I Go to Boston

And I found myself thinking that I was looking at Missouri through the eyes of a boy who had become acquainted with nature twenty years earlier in Curryville. The Missouri farms were mechanized; the food I ate in the dining car left disagreeable deposits of metal on my tongue. From seed to harvest, the produce of the Western farms passed through chill hands of steel, until it went at length into machines which crushed its goodness out. I hungered for the taste of the simple, flavorous food of my childhood. I think it was then that I resolved one day to go back to the farm.

Except that the tour left me impoverished, I felt that it had been successful. I had given it all the professional finish I could devise. My programs were fastidiously printed on good paper; I hired well-tuned pianos everywhere — at a hardly warrantable cost, because I seldom got a fee of more than fifty dollars — and I had an accompanist traveling with me. I had scarcely hoped, from the beginning, to make very much above my expenses, but I was not prepared to find it so hard to collect money I had honestly earned, and thus to make both ends meet. In my innocence I was unable to deal with a few unscrupulous agents who withheld my fees, in whole or in part, and made it impossible for me to pay my way from the receipts of the tour.

At home in Boston, just before midsummer, Ma was distressed to learn that my brother Jesse had re-enlisted in the Navy. I had urged him to come live with us, in 1916, so that he might be with Mother when I was away from home; but with the country at war, he had grown restless for the sea. I was of conscript age myself and had registered for the draft, but because I was the head of a family I was put into Class B5, from which I was never called up. Instead, I spent several months singing at military camps from Massachusetts to Georgia.

IV

In the winter of 1918 I started out on another transcontinental tour which covered, with additions, about the same ground as the first. I sang under Negro auspices, I made my own traveling arrangements, and I took my mother with me again because I could not bear to leave her behind. Before we started out she said to me: "Son, I still don't believe in this yere concert business, but since you are fixin' to go on with it, I am goin' to axe you to do one thing to make your old mother happy. When you have made good somewheres, get out. Don't hang around and kill the fine impression you have made." In these days, when publicity bears almost no relationship to the art it celebrates, Ma's advice seems conservative. Nevertheless, I have tried to follow it.

I Go to Boston

On that second obscure tour, I was invited to sing at a benefit given by a white congregation in Santa Monica. I sang a spiritual called "My Soul Is a Witness," a sung sermon I had learned in my childhood from a Negro preacher who had a knack of putting whole chapters of the Bible into memorable poetic form. It begins with the theme, "My soul is a witness for my Lord," and goes on to recite examples of "witnessing" in the Old Testament and the Gospels.

You read in the Bible and you'll understan',
Methuselah was the oldest man.
He lived nine hundred and sixty-nine,
He died and went to Heaven, Lord, in due time.
He was a witness for my Lord.

You read again and you'll understan',
Samson was the strongest man.
Samson went out at one time
And killed a thousand of the Philistines.
Delilah fooled Samson, this we know,
For the Holy Bible tells us so.
She shaved his head as clean as your han',
And his strength became as a common man.
That's another witness for my Lord.

Joshua was the son of Nun,
The Lord was with him till the work was done.
He opened the window and began to look out,
The ram's horn blew and the children did shout.

Angel Mo' and Her Son, Roland Hayes

The children did shout till the hour of seven,
The wall fell down and God heard it in heaven.

Dan'el was a Hebrew chile,
He went and prayed to his God for a while.
The king at once for Dan'el did sen',
And put him down in the lion's den.
But the Lord sent an angel the lion for to keep,
And Dan'el lay down and went to sleep.
That's another witness for my Lord.

There was a man, a Pharisee,
His name was Nicodemus, and he didn't believe.
The same came to the Lord by night,
He wanted to be led by the human sight.
Jesus told Nicodemus, as a frien',
That he must be born again.
Nicodemus asked him, he desired to know,
How can a man be born when he is ol'?
Marvel not, man, if you want to be wise,
Repent and believe and be baptize'.
Then you'll be a witness for my Lord.

I had sung this song only in Negro churches, before this time, and I was chagrined to discover, when I had sung half my way through its considerable length, that it seemed to be making very little impression upon my well-groomed white audience. Of the whole company of people there, only my mother was a practitioner of the primitive and highly emotional religion which had produced those sermons in song; and she, great soul, under the compulsion of deep religious feeling, stood up in the midst of that fashionable assembly and called out, in a clear and ringing voice, "Hallelujah! I'm a witness, too."

It was as though she had touched a match to a resinous torch. The hall became suddenly luminous, with the light of feeling come out of its dark hiding place, and at the end there was a fury of applause, a kind of manual Amen.

After the concert an elderly gentleman of aristocratic bearing came to me and said, "Mr. Hayes, you seem to me to sing with all the art of the masters I have heard, and yet with some new emotional quality of your own. I wish you would tell me how you have come by that special quality."

Now I had met with so much more of curiosity than of complimentary attention in such circles that I was a little inclined, I fear, to carry a chip on my shoulder. I drew myself up and said, "Sir, I suppose I have gone through about the same kind of training the white artists have had." The man declined to be put off by my airs. He suggested a meeting the following morning. All night I wondered what in the world he could have in his mind to say to me. At breakfast under a palm tree with my mother, in the morning, I told her what the man had said. I asked her whether she thought it was possible that there really was something unusual in my voice, something that the voices of white people did not have.

"Do you suppose," I said, "that I have been trying to turn myself into a white artist, instead of making the most of what I was born with?"

"I am glad you are finding yourself out, son," said my mother. "I knowed what was what all the time, but I wasn't going to tell you. Now go ahead and work hard and be your own man."

And that, in substance, was what the gentleman wanted to tell me, when he spoke to me for a few moments after breakfast — completing the revelation which set me upon my proper course.

In the midst of my studies in Boston I had not, thank God, lost my respect for my racial origins. I had simply added a new culture to an old one. But I was breaking ground, I had no pattern to follow, and I had been suffering from a racial habit of imitation. I had been working in a cloud of depression because my voice had not come out as "white" as, in the beginning, I must have hoped it would. Now I swore I would use the "rich purplish red" voice that Nature had given me. I felt a great release from nervous tension, and at the same time a kind of exaltation. I felt I could be what no white artist could ever be: I could be myself, sole, personal, unique.

I Go to Boston

While Stephen Graham was in this country studying Negro life in preparation for his book, *Children of
the Slaves*, he visited Mound Bayou, a wholly Negro
city in Mississippi. There he talked, as he describes it,
with one of the fathers of that experimental community,
an ancient, coal-black philosopher who said to him, "We
are trying here in Mound Bayou to understand the
beauty of being black." When I read the book in London in 1921, I felt I had found a motto for my career:
to understand the beauty of a black voice.

We stayed in California until the end of 1919, the
unholy year of race riots in Middle Western and Southern cities with large colored populations. It was said
at the time that one of the causes of the riots was re-
sentment over unequal treatment accorded to Negro
soldiers during the World War. It had been difficult
then, as it is even now — although discrimination today
is somewhat less arbitrary — for Negroes to take posi-
tions of dignity and honor in the armed services. Such
black men as were allowed to enlist, or were drafted,
were not often given a part in the manlier arts of war.
Many a brave colored boy called for a gun and was
given a spade; and when he came home after the war, he
did not try to cover up his hurt.

As soon as it was convenient to travel in public again,
we went back to Boston, and within a few weeks my

Angel Mo' and Her Son, Roland Hayes

brother John died of inflammatory rheumatism. Ma grieved over his death. He had just been ordained at the People's Baptist Church in Boston, the only one of Ma's sons to take the evangelical way she had laid out for all of us. Now that I had my heart set on going to Africa, to find my balance, I was relieved when Robert and Doll came to Boston to take John's place near my mother. They had left behind them in Los Angeles, in a cemetery called Mothersheart, the body of their only child, and I hoped my brother and my mother would be able to comfort each other.

Early in 1920 I had an engagement which added eleven hundred dollars to my bank account and made it possible for me to set out for Europe: eleven brand-new one hundred dollar bills presented to me in a leather and gold wallet, in the crowded and brilliant Green Room of the Belasco Theater in Washington. That was my first fee in four figures. Ten years earlier, Miss Lulu Vere Childers paid me thirty-five dollars to sing in "The Messiah" at Howard University, in the national capital, and that was my first paid appearance outside of Boston during my student days. It was a long ten years between my modest debut in Washington and the fabulous concert of which I speak: as long as the professional life of many a singer. And yet mine had scarcely begun.

CHAPTER FIVE

I Look at a King

I SAILED for England on the twenty-third day of April, 1920, on the first lap of a journey to Africa which I have not yet completed. I had fifteen hundred dollars in my pocket, after depositing an equal sum in a bank account for my mother. I had given her a checkbook and explained how to use it; but it was characteristic of her that she never withdrew a penny of the money. When I came back from Europe after she died, I found a hundred dollars laid away in a stocking in her trunk, saved up out of what she had earned beyond the small cost of her living. My little fund for her had not been touched. In spite of my entreaties, Ma had never given up her lifelong occupation. She laundered aprons and towels for doctors and dentists, collecting and delivering afoot, in snow and rain, in and out of season; and in addition she washed and mended for many a poor colored boy at Harvard College.

"This is my little mite for raising our people up," she would say.

Ma divided the colored race into two groups, Christian folks and "vagabon's," and she was always ready to lend a hand to anyone who professed to belong to the first category.

We sailed, Lawrence Brown and I, on the *S.S. Mauretania*, the fastest ship afloat. As first-class passengers we found ourselves in a somewhat anomalous position. If we spared the ship's staff a good deal of embarrassment, it was because both of us were seasick most of the time. At Southampton there was a little trouble about my passport. I was listed as a musician, and the immigration officials wanted to know if I proposed to give concerts for money. I had to say that I would if I could, but I explained that I had come to England primarily to study and meant to go on presently to Africa.

We taxied all over London, looking for a hotel that would take us in, and then, having spent all the money we could afford, we explored remoter districts on foot. Finally we reached a neighborhood with a sprinkling of Negro families, and there we were directed to Dusi Mohammed Ali, an African who lived in St. John's Wood. Mohammed installed us in a pair of rooms at a guinea a week apiece and went out to find a concert agent for me.

Messrs. Ibbs and Tillett of Hanover Square got a Local Board permit from Whitehall and presented me, within a month, at a small concert in Aeolian Hall in

I Look at a King

Bond Street. They paid the rent and gave me a moderate amount of publicity for the sum of sixty guineas, which was considerably more than I took in. I gave recitals every month from May to August in that year, and three more during the autumn season, and by the end of the year I had scarcely a shilling to my name. I had many friends and good prospects, but no paying engagements in sight.

My reputation in England was ultimately built up on hundreds of personal associations with people of high and low degree, rich and poor, musicians and writers, city men and lords. There came to my first London concert the Virginian wife of an Englishman, a Mrs. Fairfax, who had seen one of my announcements on a bulletin board at Aeolian Hall and vaguely wandered in. Reminded of home, she said, she had wept through the afternoon. She came to the artists' room to see me. "All England shall hear you," she promised. I met Miss Myra Hess and spent a day with her and her mother in their garden in the country. I came to know Ezra Pound, who was then writing for one of the London journals. He gave me copies of Marjory Kennedy-Fraser's arrangements of the songs of the Hebrides, and to please him — for he liked the unaccompanied singing of early songs and folkloric music — I learned to sing them without the piano. Mme. Helen Hopekirk of Boston later wrote an accompaniment, with bagpipe melodies, for Mrs. Fraser's poem, "To People Who Have Gardens," a song which I still sing every year.

Many people interested themselves in my African project. Chief Oluwa of Lagos and his entourage, in London negotiating for a better contract between the British Government and the Nigerian people, presented me with an illuminated invitation to visit them; and Sir Harry Hamilton Johnston, whose African explorations took him into the interior of Tunisia, wrote me amusing but discouraging letters about travel "in the wilds of Africa." A talented painter, Sir Harry used to exhibit his African pictures at the Royal Academy, and he liked to show sketches of the purple okapi he had discovered — *Ocapia johnstoni*, the jungle-loving, giraffe-like descendant of an animal family inhabiting the Congo in prehistoric times.

But for all the goodness of our friends, Brown and I continued to live precariously in the early months of 1921. The small fees I collected for singing at occasional At-Homes would hardly have stayed our hunger if Roger Quilter, the democratic son of an English earl, had not made free disposition to us of the resources of his well-stocked kitchen.

There were times when I was dreadfully homesick. Much of the time I was wretched and ill, and I wanted a glimpse of my mother. One day I wrote to her, in a particularly lonely moment. "Dear Mother," I said, "I love you dearly. Tell me if you do not also love me so." Days passed, and I followed in my mind the movements of letter-bearing ships at sea. At length I received her reply: "Roland, dear son, if you don't know by now whether or not I love you, I won't enlighten you by telling you so." She had never spoiled me at home and she did not propose to pamper me now that I was abroad, however much my spirits sagged.

It was about that time that I met Stephen Graham, whose book, *Children of the Slaves*, was newly published. He invited me to a party at which he read aloud from his work.

"Now listen to this paragraph, Mr. Hayes," he said, after a half hour's reading, "and tell me what you think of it. It sums the whole book up."

He slapped his thigh and read out the following lines: —

> The Southerner has made the Negro a pair of boots and he says they fit very well. The Negro says they don't fit. But the Southerner says he'll risk salvation on it — he made the boots, and he knows his trade. The Negro, however, has to wear them.

One of the guests at Mr. Graham's party was the Reverend Hugh B. Chapman who, in days past, had spoken out against the betrothal of the Duke of York to the Princess Victoria Mary, and for ten or twelve years thereafter had been banished to the slums. Now restored to favor, he was chaplain of the Royal Chapel of the Savoy, the priestly duties of which he had undertaken in addition to his work amongst the poor. When I related to the Honorable Helen Douglas some of the great things His Reverence promised me that night he would do for me, she said, "Padre can get away with anything, the old devil."

Padre was as good as his word. On the seventeenth of March, by his appointment, I sang a recital of Negro music in the Royal Chapel, including the sorrowful "Steal Away to Jesus" that my great-grandfather used to sing. At the end of the program the organist played the "Largo" from the "New World Symphony" and the Chaplain preached and read some prayers. There seems to have been no criticism of this event because it was not a Prayer Book occasion. But three days later, on Palm Sunday, I sang the spiritual "Were You There?" at Vespers in the Chapel. I wore choir vestments and stood in the chancel and sang unaccompanied. One of the newspapers thought my part in a stated service was un-English and un-Anglican. I was distressed, but at lunch in the chantry on the following day, Padre told me that if I would be patient I should see that something good would come of my singing, in spite of the talk. He always wrote and spoke to me with unextinguishable enthusiasm and apostolic love.

At last Messrs. Ibbs and Tillett, feeling that I was ready for a concert at Wigmore Hall, engaged that celebrated chamber for the night of April 21, 1921. Since I had no money to pay the customary guarantee, they advertised the recital out of their own funds and persuaded the Wigmore manager to let me sing on tick. Music as an art has long rested uneasily upon the tough substructure of the music business, and it was partly because my managers were making unheard-of concessions that I felt honor-bound to work for a great success. I worked beyond my own strength and judgment, actually, because both purse and reputation were at stake.

Soon after the concert was announced, an order from the Prime Minister, Mr. David Lloyd George, closed public buildings in the interest of saving fuel, all England being then harassed by strikes in the coal-mining regions. I practically lost my mind. I was hungry, my spirits were low, the weather was stormy and cold, and I came down with pneumonia.

Shortly before the twenty-first of the month the strikes were stayed for a few weeks and the theaters and concert halls were reopened. I instructed my agents

Angel Mo' and Her Son, Roland Hayes

to go ahead with my recital, although my physician had ordered me to give it up. I reached the old-fashioned ninth-day pulmonary crisis on the morning of the appointed day. I was running a high temperature, but I still felt the concert must go on. If it was a matter of life and death with me as a man, as the doctor warned me, it was also a conflict between the death and the survival of the artist.

I sent Lawrence Brown out to do some errands and persuaded my good friend Mohammed to help me get up out of bed. He dressed me and wrapped me up and had me ready to be bundled into a taxi when Brown returned. Lawrence, when he saw me, turned white under his black skin.

Wigmore Hall was full when we arrived. The manager was wringing his hands because I was late, but he grew hysterical when he saw the condition I was in. I had to be carried upstairs. I asked an attendant to place a chair between the piano and the door from the artists' room. Nearly unconscious when I made my entrance, I managed to reach out and grasp the back of the chair for support. I slid along the curve of the piano until I reached a point where I could stop to bow to my audience. Brown followed me, shaking with fear and momentarily awaiting my collapse.

I opened my program with "*Nimm mich dir zu eigen*

(*134*)

hin," from Bach's Sixty-fifth Cantata. I had not the slightest feeling; I was resigned to any dreadful end. I only thought, "This may be the last act of my life." I knew the air thoroughly, of course, and I could sing it almost automatically. Indeed, I had been rehearsing mentally, as my habit is, through my illness. Yet I had no physical force to muster; my body was as weak as water. Only spiritual forces were active within me, and these of themselves produced words and notes and tones.

At the end of the first group of songs I walked out alone, like a man in a trance, past the piano, past the chair, and through the door into the Green Room. When I returned to the stage for the second group, I had no feeling of sickness or infirmity. I reached out to my audience and gathered it into myself. The metropolitan critics, in the morning, informed the British public that Roland Hayes was a musician of the first water.

The next afternoon, while I was taking tea in Roger Quilter's house, a telephone call was relayed to me from Messrs. Ibbs and Tillett. I knew that Mohammed would have given them Quilter's number only under the most urgent necessity, and I went trembling to the telephone, expecting to hear that my concert had brought about my financial ruin. Mr. Tilbrook, the treasurer of that organization, was on the wire.

"Has Mrs. Fairfax told you the news?" he asked.

"No," said I, "what news?"

"I think I should wait for her to tell you," said he.

"Do tell me now," I pleaded.

"Well," said he, "if I do tell you, you must not repeat it just yet. You have been commanded to sing before Their Majesties in Buckingham Palace."

I fainted dead away.

II

On the following day, April 23, only two days after my Wigmore Hall concert, Brown and I dressed ourselves in the prescribed attire and waited for a royal limousine to drive up to our door. We were met at Buckingham Palace by the Master of the Household, who escorted us to an antechamber where he coached us in the manners expected of us at the presentation. We then went into the White Drawing Room, in the company of some of the lords and ladies of the Household, and anxiously awaited the entrance of the Royal Family. Finally a lackey thrust open a door and announced the King.

I had been instructed to rise, make a deep bow, and remain at half-mast until Their Majesties were seated. I had supposed that I should then be ceremoniously presented, at which time, according to the book, I would have held a deep bow until I should have been spoken to. But the King himself upset these carefully ordered arrangements with a wave of his hand.

"There will be no formality today," he said, as he came into the Drawing Room. "I propose to meet Mr. Hayes as man to man. Present Mr. Hayes to me now."

I stepped forward to make my bow. The King advanced and offered his hand. I was then presented to the Queen, the Princess Mary, and the Duke of York, the present King of England. I sang to them for half an hour, from a small approved program of European, English, and Negro songs. Their Majesties demanded more, and altogether I remained with them for nearly two hours.

I had not expected to be engaged in conversation with the King and Queen, and I was astonished when His Majesty, after my first group, abruptly asked me if I knew what it was that had caused the first rift between the British and American people.

"Your Majesty," I said, "I'm afraid I am deficient in history. I cannot remember anything before the Boston Tea Party."

"Yes," said the King, "that is what most people would say, but the fact is, feeling was first aroused by our own English Quakers, who spoke against slavery in the American colonies."

Angel Mo' and Her Son, Roland Hayes

After the second group Queen Mary asked me what came next on the program. Having lately read, in the annals of the Court, of Her Majesty's attendance at a minstrel show, I told her that I was about to sing some traditional religious songs, of which she had perhaps heard syncopated versions in the music hall. I explained that scholars believed that some of the Negro music was as much as a hundred and fifty years old. The texts, I said, were principally from Biblical sources, rephrased in common language by people who could not read; and the music had rhythmical qualities and sometimes a peculiar system of intervals which showed that it was based on tribal music, handed down from African days. I recalled that the first written records of the spirituals had been made only after the War Between the States, and that some of those early versions had been sung in London by the Fisk Jubilee Singers exactly half a century before. I explained that I myself sang the words as I had learned them during my childhood in Georgia.

Minstrel singers years ago took over the old secular plantation songs, and after that there was a tendency to secularize the religious music for popular consumption. "Blues," which had been invented only about ten years before I went to London, were freely drawn from both secular and religious sources. Such composers as

I Look at a King

Harry T. Burleigh and J. Rosamond Johnson have spent their lives trying to recapture and preserve the original form and spirit of the songs which our forebears created in the service of God.

On my way home from Buckingham Palace I sent a cable to my mother to say that I had sung before the King and Queen. I heard from my friends that Ma was immensely pleased, but she herself, fearful lest I be swollen with pride, simply replied, "Remember who you are and give credit where it is due."

When the story of the command performance appeared in the Boston newspapers, reporters flocked out to call on her. "We have come to hear the story from you, Mrs. Hayes," they said.

"What story?" asked my mother.

"Don't you know that your son sang to the King and Queen of England yesterday?"

"Yes, I knowed it before any of you all knowed it," said my mother. "Now you all go along. My irons is hot, and if I don't get on with my work, my boys won't have their shirts."

She allowed herself to be photographed only on the condition that the camera men would not interfere with her ironing. The reporters trooped out into the kitchen behind her and plied her with questions. Ma went placidly on with her work. She was photographed at the ironing board and Harry Sutton made her portrait from a print. Today, that portrait makes a holy shrine of my Brookline house.

I heard from many sources in London that the Queen continued to speak of me frequently. Some three years later I sang at Lady Harcourt's house in Mayfair, at Queen Mary's request, and I was greeted there by every diplomat present except the American ambassador. The Queen inquired what I had been doing over the three years lately past, and what my plans were for the future. I told her that I had been engaged to sing with the Royal Philharmonic Society in Madrid the next season, and I have always supposed it was at her suggestion that I was commanded at that time to sing before Queen Mother Cristina of Spain.

Early in May of the year 1921, Dame Nellie Melba came to London to sing a farewell concert in Royal ___rt Hall. At her reception by the King and Queen, Their Majesties took pains to recommend me to her. Thus it came to pass that on the following Saturday, Roger Quilter and I motored over to Maidenhead to lunch at the house where she was staying. Madame Melba walked me up and down the garden for an hour, telling me what the King and Queen had said, and proposed a party for me at the house she had hired in the West End. Her establishment in London was always overrun, she said, with artists from the everywhere.

I sat next to Melba at lunch in the garden, and I remember being embarrassed because she and Quilter shouted ribald stories at each other, down the length of the luncheon table: for that was my first intimate glimpse as a seated guest, so to speak, of fashionable English society.

After lunch, Dame Nellie asked me to sing "A Furtive Tear," from Donizetti's opera *"L'Elisir d'Amore."* When I asked her why she had chosen that aria, she said that she thought we might as well begin at the top. Jean de Reszké, whom she called the greatest singer of all time, had sung it inimitably, she said.

"If you can approach de Reszké's presentation of the vocal line of that song . . . just the *entrée*, if you like . . . I will know that you are a great artist. It is the severest test a singer can take."

I was not a little apprehensive at having to re-create a difficult aria on the spur of the moment, although I had sung it frequently at home. I said, "I will sing it for you, but only in my own way. I have never heard it sung by anyone else."

The air begins *pianissimo* on a high note. The attack must come without effort, like a breath out of the silence, with no indication of the vocal mechanics. What follows is written along a long, sustained vocal line which must remain intact, and at the end there is a cadenza which the voice has to carry without accompaniment.

I had not finished the first phrase, had scarcely sung two bars, when Melba jumped up from her chair and ran to me with outstretched arms.

"No one, not even de Reszké, has ever made such a divine entry into that song," she said.

Trying not to look distracted or embarrassed, I began the aria again and sang it through. I confess to a moment of great pleasure when I saw Melba dissolved in tears. I sang on for perhaps an hour, some of the *Lieder* and some of the songs of my childhood. Melba liked "Swing Low, Sweet Chariot," and a few months later I recorded it for her and sent the disk to her home in Melbourne, whence she had taken her name.

Sir Edward Elgar and Fritz Kreisler were amongst the throng of guests at Melba's party up in London a few days later. Dame Nellie presented me to the company with a speech in which she told about the honor the King and Queen had paid me, and asked me to sing the Donizetti aria again. Out of the quiet that succeeded the conclusion of the cadenza, Melba came rustling up to the piano, and with a theatrical flourish made me a present of a signed photograph.

"Mr. Hayes," she said, "you are a great artist, and so says the King."

I Look at a King

Royal recognition and Melba's patronage opened a great many doors to me. Lady Astor invited me to sing at Cliveden almost immediately. Lloyd George was present, together with M.P.'s and lords of the Opposition. After dinner, which I took privately with Lawrence Brown, I sang a group of spirituals, such as "Bye an' Bye," "Deep River," and "Go Down, Moses." When I was presented to the Prime Minister, he said, "I am grateful to you for singing 'Go Down, Moses,' for it will help me to meet the miners tomorrow." I could not help being amused by the thought of his probable exhortation to the miners — "Go down, Moses, go down to your mines" — in a voice like that of Jehovah Himself.

I sang frequently at Lord Astor's house in St. James's Square the following summer, also at Cliveden. On one occasion the guests at the town house were members of a delegation which had come from Virginia for the unveiling of a statute of George Washington. I had asked Lady Astor whether my presence might not be an embarrassment for all of us.

"Not at all," she said. "I shall make it plain that you are coming, and if there is anyone who doesn't want to meet you, he can stay away." At the reception she took me by the arm, led me about amongst the visiting Virginians, and introduced me most disarmingly.

Angel Mo' and Her Son, Roland Hayes

I have saved a budget of letters from St. James's Square, The Hoe in Plymouth, and from Cliveden in Buckinghamshire, some of them from secretaries writing about professional engagements and enclosing checks, but many of them written or dictated by Lady Astor herself. In one of them she speaks of a little Negro girl who is her namesake, and whose mother she loves as dearly as one of her own sisters.

"Color does not matter, does it," she writes, "so long as the heart is alright."

In 1929 she wrote from Cliveden to say that I had been her only "musical experiment," and that she had done for me only what her mother, who loved music and loved my race, would have liked her to do. I wept a little when I read the lines: "So, you go on being inspired by your Mother — as I go on being inspired by mine."

I thought of the warm, impulsive woman I had come to admire in England when I read about her in a dispatch from England early in the present war. One of her servants described her gallantry during a Nazi raid on Plymouth: —

My lady made us all join her in prayer when one bomb blew the front door in, and another the back of the house, while a third threw an automobile onto the roof. Then the Germans began to drop fire bombs.

I Look at a King

My lady sprang to her feet. "Where in the hell is the fire bucket?" she cried, as she led us all to the roof.

III

It was very much on my mind, while I was in England, that I had need to perfect my diction and accent in French and German and to learn more about the great traditions which prescribe the stylistic performance of the various musical *genres*. Back home in Boston, Mrs. Hubbard, the wife of my teacher and a musician of impeccable taste, had coached me in languages and in the interpretation of European songs; an Italian youth from the North End had tutored me for two years in exchange for lessons; and Mr. Hubbard himself had taught me to sing Continental music in the language in which it had been written. By the time I went to England in 1920, my teacher at home had already laid the musical groundwork for my career. Indeed, he had made me a singer. But there were several composers whose work I had not yet approached from the inside: Brahms was one of them and Bach was another. It was a fortunate circumstance, then, that in the summer of 1921 I was introduced by the Honorable Helen Douglas to Sir George Henschel, a pupil of Brahms. I had heard about Sir George in Boston, where he was revered as the first conductor of the Symphony

Angel Mo' and Her Son, Roland Hayes

Orchestra. Miss Douglas, who always wore silvery, shimmering gowns and draped herself with loops of jewels — achieving thereby an unmistakable aura of royalty — had taken great pains to bring us together.

I went regularly for some months to Sir George's studio, The Red House, in Kensington, and the choleric composer shook his pointed beard at me until I acquired the vocal refinement exacted by the music of Brahms. I also learned some of his own songs, scholarly compositions somewhat in the manner of his master, and liked especially his setting for Blake's poem, "Little Lamb, Who Made Thee?" Sir George complimented me with a dedication to his setting for the Twenty-third Psalm, written on his eightieth birthday.

In June of that year, in the midst of my serious studies, I took a little vacation in Paris. I was not yet quite ready to venture to sing in German and French on the Continent, but I hoped to sow the seed for a harvest of concerts a few months later. As it turned out, my visit was only an episode in a sentimental journey which left me ill in body, depressed in spirit, poor in pocket, and no whit advanced upon my chosen way.

We registered, Brown and I, at a good hotel, in an atmosphere in which embarrassment was refreshingly absent, and I went out at once to call on Wesley Howard, the Negro violinist. After tea, the Howards charged a young *Parisienne* of their acquaintance with taking me back to my rooms. The young woman told the taxicab driver to take us to our destination by way of the Bois de Boulogne, and as we drove along through the early evening, she spoke of a fashionable restaurant deep in the shady woods. If Monsieur would like to see it, she said, it would be her pleasure to point it out. She was further inspired to wonder, as we drew up to the door of a glittering pavilion, whether Monsieur would like to partake of food in that chic environment. She gave orders to the driver, prodded me out of the cab, and led the way through mirrored corridors into a hall of such elegance and luxury as I had never supposed I should see with my own eyes.

We were surrounded instantly by a cordon of uniformed officials whose function, I guessed, was to prevent our escape until we had been sufficiently plundered. I began nervously to finger the single two-hundred-franc note I had in my pocket, but I was quite unable to resist the hierarchy of gilded waiters who led us to a table in a bower of potted chestnut trees. The headwaiter — he could hardly have been less than Cardinal amongst his kind — handed us a menu written in antique script, with flourishes of violet ink. My companion ordered food enough to satisfy the hunger of half a dozen starving musicians, while my own appetite froze within me. I watched her consume one delicacy upon another, and anxiously scanned the menu to calculate the mounting charges. I had counted as far as a hundred francs when she demanded the *carte du vin*. While she made her leisurely choice of a vintage claret, my straining ears seemed to catch the clocking of the meter in the taxicab outside.

Thus Mademoiselle polished off the several courses of her dinner, devouring my portions along with hers, and proceeded, glass after lingering glass, to drink the contents of a mustily expensive bottle.

At length, after coffee, I received the bill from the hands of a personage whom I might easily have mistaken for a director of the Bank of France. I recovered my speech only to protest a staggering total which would have left me with only twenty-five of my two hundred francs. My cicerone seized the account and said without stopping to look at it, "But, of course, Monsieur, the *addition* is correct." She took the small notes returned to me in change and distributed them amongst a bevy of waiters and busboys.

The taximeter read exactly eighty-five francs, and so far as I knew, we still had a long way to go. I pretended that I had forgotten something at Wesley Howard's apartment and asked to be taken there. At some point in the city the cab came to a stop and my

I Look at a King

vis-à-vis left me, with a bright smile and a debonair *adieu.* Something told me I should never see her again.

When I returned to my hotel, with a few centimes left over from a hundred francs I borrowed from the Howards, I discovered that two white Americans had seen Lawrence Brown in the lobby and ordered the management, which had received us so hospitably, to put us out. On our journey back to London, we swore that we would never set foot in Paris again. If I had ever dared to tell my mother the story of that visit, she would have said that I had been rightly served. I had not been watchful of the "physical man."

In the end, I returned to Paris sooner than my first distastes for that city would have promised. Ernest Newman, the music critic of the *Manchester Guardian* and *The Times* of London, came to one of my concerts, at the end of 1921, and published the extravagant opinion that the only singer he really liked at the moment was the new Negro tenor. It appeared that Joseph Salmon, the 'cellist, had only been waiting to be reassured of a conviction privately arrived at, and within a few days he invited me to come to Paris to sing at soirées which he undertook to arrange.

I had met M. Salmon at the house of Mr. Norman O'Neill, the composer, who had written some songs for me. The night Salmon was present I sang a short program of Handel, Purcell, and Schubert; two songs from Roger Quilter's Shakespeare cycle, one of which, the "Take Oh Take Those Lips Away," was written especially for me; and some spirituals, of which the last was my great-grandfather's story of the Crucifixion, "He Never Said a Mumberlin' Word."

When I finished singing I was astonished to meet only silence. There was no applause; not a word was spoken. The room was nearly dark; my audience seemed to have vanished while my eyes were closed. I saw only Quilter, who moved toward me like a spirit. I asked him what had happened to his guests.

"They are in the dark corners, hiding behind their handkerchiefs," he whispered, with an exaggeration of his habitual stammering. "The English are ashamed to show their emotions, you know."

M. Salmon came up to me at last, handkerchief in hand, and said, "Mr. Hayes, I'm an old man now, and I cannot expect to live very long. You must come to France while I'm still alive. I shall introduce you to all Paris."

I was enchanted with the reception I met with in Paris during my second visit, in the spring of 1922. M. Salmon had promised me five concerts with *cachet* at once, but presently I found myself with twenty-five or thirty invitations to sing in great houses. I had the patronage of Bourbons and Rothschilds, of the Princesse de Colloredo-Mansfeld, the Duc and Duchesse de La Rochefoucauld de Bisaccia, the Comtesse Bourtourline, the Portuguese Baronesse d'Itajuba, and the famous Mme. Tata. In Paris, it was no crime to be black.

There were two very special guests at a party which M. Salmon gave for me, Mme. Alexandre Dumas and the Comtesse Anna de Noailles. Mme. Dumas invited my host and me to dine with her on the third day following, and after dinner she took me into a small drawing room where she had laid out a quantity of Dumas photographs.

"No doubt you have heard all sorts of stories about the origin of the Dumas family," she said. "Now I am going to tell you the truth."

She picked up a portrait of a tall, soldierly, dark-skinned man in shooting costume.

"What do you think of that?" she asked.

"He certainly looks like a black man to me," I said.

"And so he was," she replied. "Now you may tell whomever you meet that a Dumas *vrai* told you that Dumas *père* was a Negro."

Mme. Dumas explained that her father-in-law had given his children the name of his mother, a Negro woman of San Domingo, because his father, a French nobleman, had never recognized him. That same day there was delivered to my hotel that identical photograph of Alexandre Dumas *père*, with the autograph of my hostess.

The Comtesse Anna de Noailles, who was born a Rumanian princess of the family Brancovan, was a poet and woman of fashion. Women copied what she wore and men repeated what she said. No party was complete without her and she obliged by going everywhere. At a *salon* at M. Leon Balby's — he was the publisher of *Le Transigeant* — the Comtesse was in such high spirits that she could not contain herself. When it came time for me to sing, Mme. Balby introduced me, my accompanist played the prelude to Handel's "Where'er You Walk," and the Comtesse chattered at the top of her voice. I waited a little while and then, because I did not like the night-club atmosphere, I retired to the dressing room. I explained to M. Balby, who followed after me, that I could not sing to his guests if they would not listen to me.

"It is the Comtesse de Noailles," said M. Balby. "I will speak to her. She has a heart of gold. Please don't go."

In a moment the Comtesse rushed in to apologize.

"How could you think I would do anything to hurt your feelings?" she said. "I was only speaking of your wonderful singing."

I Look at a King

"Thank you, my dear Comtesse," I replied. "I shall be delighted to sing for you if you will be so good as to talk about it afterwards."

"I agree with pleasure," she said, "and I will kill anyone who dares to make a sound while you are singing."

We became great friends and the Comtesse sent me copies of her verses, one of which Reginald Boardman, who has accompanied me since Percival Parham died, has lately set to music: —

Pourtant tu t'en iras un jour de moi, jeunesse,
Tu t'en iras tenant l'amour entre tes bras,
La bouche pleine d'ombre et les yeux pleins de cris.
Je te rappellerai d'une clameur si forte
Que pour ne plus m'entendre "appeler de la sorte,"
La mort entre ses mains prendra mon cœur meurtri.

Through letters of introduction from friends in London I met Frederick Delius, who had a villa near Fontainebleau. He told me, at one time and another, something of the story of his life: how he ran away to grow oranges in Florida and ended up teaching music in Virginia; and how his friend, Edvard Grieg, persuaded his parents to let him go on with his musical studies at home. Upon his return to Leipzig, he wrote the orchestral suite called "Florida." When I knew him, he was crippled and nearly blind, but he lived on to attend, in

1929, a festival for which Sir Thomas Beecham ordered the performance of nearly all of the composer's work.

I was also taken to meet André Messager, a pupil of Saint-Saëns. I sang the "Dream Song" for him, from the "Manon" of Massenet, and he offered to write an opera especially for me. I told him that in America I had sung opera only behind a movie screen, and explained that my teachers had long since discouraged me from trying to make my way against the prejudices of the operatic world. As a matter of fact, I had become generally persuaded of the greater refinement of oratorio and concert music, and no longer wished the pattern of my life to be changed.

Debussy dedicated his *"Pelléas et Mélisande"* to Messager, who first conducted that opera; but it was not Messager who made me a convert, for a time, to the Debussy religion. Roger Quilter had given me a letter which led to my introduction to Gabriel Fauré, the organist at the Madeleine, and it was Fauré, the teacher of many of the younger European composers, including Ravel, Florent Schmidt, and Roger-Ducasse, who introduced me to the music of the Impressionist. He told me that when Massenet, Debussy's teacher, saw the first version of the cantata *"L'Enfant Prodigue,"* with which, in a later form, Debussy won the *Prix de Rome,* he was shocked by some of the advanced passages and blue-penciled most of the modernity clean out of them. I have gone through masses of manuscript, hoping to find the original music, but I am still obliged to use the printed version, in which Debussy is dissolved in Massenet.

Fauré invited me to sing in his studio. I produced a sheaf of his own songs, in some of which I had found interpretative difficulties, and asked for counsel. He communicated to me, first and last, something of his own taste for classical refinement. He explained that he had chosen his texts carefully, from the corpus of French poetry, and asked me not to add anything to the settings he had provided for them; in short, I could do no better — I was reminded of Miss Robinson! — than to follow carefully the composer's indications of expression and tempo. Extemporizing additions of *rubato* or acceleration, he felt, could only produce meretricious and irrelevant effects. Fauré, the most classical of French composers himself, was devoted solely to pure music. Coming as I did from America and England, I was ripe for the ascetic discipline he gave me.

My mother would have applauded, for the sake of my soul, an episode which occurred at the end of that heartening visit to Paris. An American *princesse* invited me to wait upon her to discuss an appearance at one of her soirées. I think she must have heard a good deal about me, for I was indubitably in vogue in the city. She knew Anna de Noailles, who claimed to have made me the "measles of Paris." But my Gallic friends and critics did not habitually speak of me as a "Negro tenor," as people of other nations generally did, and it is my guess that she had not known that I was a black man until her maid was confronted by my person.

At any rate, after I had handed in my card I waited quite a long time before the lady came down to her drawing room. She was gloved and hatted and had a busy air of having much to do. She made me not a little nervous, but I sang for her, and took my leave without very much encouragement. On my way out of the house I saw my card in a wastebasket. It was just another example of the kind of thing that has happened to me now and again throughout my life, perhaps to help me "remember who I am."

CHAPTER SIX

I Take Last Leave of My Mother

IN THE FALL of 1922 I received a letter from my mother, in which she spoke, for the first time, of old age and the inevitability of death. She said she was "well as common," but she admitted that she suffered from the incurable complaint of age. Still, she said, "I feel good because the Lord let me have all the days he promised me. You must be glad for me, and not feel sad when the Lord comes to take me away. For if I am who I say I am, I will be better off. I am willing to stay as long as I can make my living. When I can't work, I want Him to take me away. I don't want to be no trouble to anyone. I am working just like I am going to stay here always, but I stand ready to die any time."

I was deeply shocked to come upon the words, a few lines later, "I can't last much longer. As I said, old age will kill me any day."

Mother was discouraged about my brother Robert,

who took after our father in respect to churchgoing. She wanted me to pray for him — if I felt I was living so I could "go to the Lord in the full assurance of faith." I suspected she had quarreled with him and had shut herself up for a time. She seemed so lonely.

I sailed from France in November to see her. I hoped to persuade her to go back to Europe with me, so that I could look after her during her last days; or at the least, I thought I might convince her, before she died, that my concert work was really a mission: dedicated, like that of a preacher, to God and religion.

We had a wonderful visit together, Mother and I. Ma came a little closer to me than she had ever been before, and I, on the other hand, learned to understand more nearly the secrets of her heart and mind. I did not expect her to talk softly to me. It was not in her nature to be sentimental. But she pleased me by showing an interest in my music. She spoke of the message of my songs and urged me again to be careful of my diction. Singing is not just an exercise of the voice and the lungs, she would say. A song without a message, a spiritual message, was only an agreeable noise to her. And she constantly reminded me, in the most persuasive way, that in the spiritual universe nothing base is tolerable.

I found her still deeply occupied with her work at home and in the church, and I was not surprised when she declined to go abroad with me. In spite of failing health, she still did washing for many Negro boys and girls — without charge, if they were earning an education — and when they brought and fetched their laundry, she would give them something to eat and encourage them to talk. She was interested in their problems and gave them sound, if often difficult, advice. There was a young musician of our name, the organist at the Ebenezer Baptist Church, who said to me, "I don't know what I would do without your mother, she gives such good counsel."

Women who had trouble keeping their houses and minding their babies would come to my mother, and she would teach them how to cook and mend and take care of their children. There was a woman who used to come from Haverhill every month. I never knew exactly what she came for, but her air of reverence in the presence of my mother made her visits seem a kind of pilgrimage. If Ma drove the truths of the Spirit home as with a brisk blow of a hammer, at least her confidants recognized the truth inherent in her speech and came back time and again for more of it. There was in her manner of speaking something of the immediacy and communicability of the Old Testament prophets. She was perfectly aware of her Christian priesthood, too, and talked with Biblical dignity.

Angel Mo' and Her Son, Roland Hayes

Mother was not much impressed by my European trophies — contracts and programs and jeweled presents from the King and Queen — but she wept a little when I told her that I had sung spirituals which she had taught me to thousands of poor creatures in the London slums; and she allowed herself to be quite won over, when, after a concert I gave on a Sunday afternoon in Symphony Hall, one of the critics wrote that I had not really sung a music-hall recital. I had, he said, conducted a religious service.

That concert had seemed to me, too, in fact, to be a religious occasion. Before I was able to make my bow, the whole audience rose to its feet in a welcome which warms my heart even as I think of it now. I prayed that I should not disappoint those generous people. On Monday morning after breakfast I showed the reviews to my mother. She read them one by one in silence, got up with a sigh from her chair, wiped her hands on her apron, and went out into the kitchen to get our midday dinner. Although she did not speak, I knew she was full of some deep feeling. I went into my room and packed my bags for a trip to New York and Washington.

When we were seated at table, in front of steaming platters of Ma's good cooking, my mother reached out and patted my hand.

I Take Last Leave of My Mother

"Well, son, I give in," she said. "I see now what you are trying to do. I'm not afraid for you any more. I see that yo' feet are on the Rock."

I asked what it was that had caused her to change her mind about me.

"I didn't feel nuthin' about yo' singin' till yesterday," she said. "Ev'ybody felt something holy then, and now I see it in the papers."

Presently it was necessary for me to go back to England. Early in the morning of January 25, 1923, I walked for the last time down the rickety stairs of the little frame house where we had a small flat. Mother said she would go down with me to the door, something she had never done before. In the dark vestibule she threw her arms around me.

"Mother," I said, "do come with me! It is not too late." Ma was silent, she held me close to her. "Then will you promise," I asked, "that you will go with me the next time I come back? I will get you a fine house in Paris."

Ma put her hands on my shoulders and looked at me out of her time-worn eyes.

"I won't be here when you come again, son," she said, "but that ain't nothin'. My days are over and yours are jest begun. I want *you* to promise *me* that when I fall down, you won't try to come back here and pick me up. You can't do me no good when I'm dead. Jes' remember this, you are the continuation of my desire. When I go, if you've been dutiful, all the best in me is going to double up in you and become a bulwark of strength. I never could do very much myself, and now I'm ol' I can't do nuthin' more — but I have always prayed the good Lord that I might do somethin' good through some of my children."

"Tell me, Mother," I said through my tears, "tell me that I can do what you want me to do."

"You are young, and can do anything," she replied. "God said, 'I call upon you, ye young men, 'cause you are strong.' Now you go on, remember who you are and reverence yo' heritage. You ain't got no cause to worry 'bout me. I'm all right. Jes' look what I have aroun' me, the whole Church is roun' about my side."

It must have been bright morning now, but I stumbled out of the house in darkness. I never saw my mother again.

I sailed that day for England, with my new secretary-valet, Howard T. Jordan, the son of some old friends from Louisville. I had eaten fried chicken many a time with the Jordans, during the months I had spent there in 1910. They had seemed to believe in me, at a moment when I had been feeling particularly friendless — after the crisis at Fisk. For the first time in my life, I was learning then, at first hand, what it was to suffer at the hands of white people, and Mrs. Jordan helped me to adjust myself to a new world. "We know that not all colored people are comic," she would say, "and neither are all white people intelligent and refined." She taught me where and how to put my trust in people of the other race.

I drew up a set of rules and regulations for the behavior of my attendant, a boy I had known since his childhood! It contained nine general orders, each with a multiplicity of specifications. The point of most of them was that he was to be, at all times and seasons, at the immediate service of his principal. As it turned out, I had ample occasion to put the young man's tactful fidelity to good use. Perhaps I bent over backwards to be irreproachable in dress and appearance, but I had definitely acquired a taste for immaculate grooming. Furthermore, I was involved in a rapidly mounting correspondence to which, in those days, I tried to give scrupulous attention. More than anything else, however, I needed a buffer, so that in the approaching days of unremitting travel I should not have to bear by myself the wear and tear of traffic with the white folks' world.

I had three months in which to get ready for my debut in Vienna, the music capital of the whole of

Europe then. I took up residence in Hampstead and went to work with my teachers, in the midst of a crowded season which Messrs. Ibbs and Tillett had arranged for me. A hundred years earlier, John Keats had quit Hampstead for Italy, a circumstance of which I learned through a letter from a man who had written to me in August 1922, when I was in Paris: "I came out to Hampstead, since I'm come to England for a day or two, hoping to see you and to trace Keats." It was from Wentworth Place in that district — friends pointed out to me the site of the house where he is supposed to have lived — that Keats, in the spring of the year in which he went to Rome, wrote to his sister of the "tightness in the Chest" which sent him off to the milder air of Italy.

I took time out that winter to hear music and to visit some of the musical landmarks. I saw the narrow brick house where Handel lived when he composed "The Messiah," which the famous Mrs. Cibber, the actress and sister of Dr. Arne, the composer, had introduced to London. The contralto arias were written for her, and the part of Galatea in "Acis and Galatea" as well. I had a sentimental attachment to the oratorio — although Handel preferred "Samson" above it — because, in a sense, I had made my professional debut in it. When I went to Dublin to sing at the Mansion House during the week of the Horse Show, I drove past Neal's Music Hall, where "The Messiah" had its first performance on April 13, 1742. Handel, ill and blind, attended a performance of that cantata in London, only a week before his death, on the Holy Saturday of 1759, having failed, so it is said of him, in willing himself to die on the Good Friday preceding.

I sang the aria "Where'er You Walk" from Handel's "Semele" in Paris in 1922 and again at Symphony Hall, Boston, in January, 1923. I used to speak of the work as an opera, but a critic in the *Amsterdam Handelsblatt* pointed out that although William Congreve had written an operatic libretto, Handel had made an oratorio out of it.

I saw a good deal, during the Hampstead season, of Samuel Coleridge-Taylor's widow and children, Hiawatha and Gwendolen, who had sent to my ship, when I sailed to America to visit my mother in 1922, a *bon voyage* basket, addressed to "Mr. Roland Hayes, the sweetest of all singers." Coleridge-Taylor's first important orchestral composition was the Ballad in A minor, written for the Gloucester Festival by order of Sir Edward Elgar; his most famous chorale is the "Hiawatha's Wedding Feast," first performed at the Royal College of Music. I had sung many of his songs in the early days at home, and I continued to sing them in London and on the Continent. In April, 1923, just before I went to Vienna, I visited his grave in Croydon and laid a wreath of flowers upon his tomb, underneath some sculptured verses composed by Alfred Noyes for his memorial.

As a result of concerts I gave in England that year — with the Streatham Philharmonic Orchestra, at one of Mr. Percy Bull's Nine-O'Clock Concerts at King's College Hall, and for At-Homes in places like Grosvenor House and Sir Philip Sassoon's mansion — I was invited to make some phonograph records. Until quite lately, I could never bring myself to repeat that experience. I had made a few disks at home, back in 1917, in order to earn a little extra money, and had set up a small distributing office on Boylston Street, in Boston, with a sales manager and a letterhead which read "Roland W. Hayes, Sole Owner" in small letters, and "Roland W. Hayes, Phonograph Records," in capitals. My best salesman was my mother, who sold a good many records to members of her church. Now, in London, I found myself under contract to make five records of spirituals, with the understanding that after my voice had been thus tested, I should be called in for a discussion of terms. The records came out very well, but the terms which were offered seemed to me to be ungenerous. I went to the manufacturer's office to recover the

I Take Last Leave of My Mother

matrixes, which somebody handed to me, together with
a pair of metal shears and an inferential nod. Although
I had not felt exactly satisfied with my disembodied
voice, I had taken some secret pleasure in listening to it,
and I hated to cut up the recordings without hearing
them again. But I accepted the scissors, sliced the metal
disks neatly in half, and went away.

I told Roger Quilter that what made me sad was
that I had sung some of the recorded songs all over
England, in the Winter Garden, at Bournemouth and
Margate, and in many of the northern and middle counties, the "colored counties" which I loved. Quilter
tried to console me by taking me to his mother's house
at Woodside in Suffolk. I was pleased with the prospect
of meeting Lady Quilter and her sister, an elderly aunt
of whom Roger gave delightful imitations, in spite of
his habit of stuttering. When it was known that I was
coming to visit, she inquired of Roger every day, "Is
Mr. Hayes married, and is his wife fond of him?"

It was nice to have friends I could go to all over
England. I could not help remembering the forlorn
beginning of my first voyage abroad. I was introduced,
just before I sailed from home in 1920, to an Englishman
who was traveling in America on an official mission.
He offered me letters of introduction to officers of the
British Museum and other "right" people, but he advised

me to make a modest entry into his country — as against my teacher, who said that unless I blew my own horn, I was not likely to make any noise. He warned me impressively about British distinctions of caste, and told me, in fact, that he was not sure he would speak to me himself in Piccadilly.

II

The immediate circumstances of my debut in Vienna did not seem, in advance, to be particularly auspicious. I had few friends there, and I could not take time out to go over and soak up the atmosphere of the city before my concert. Still, I was prepared to sing the songs of Schubert and Schumann, Brahms, Beethoven, and Wolf, and I hoped that if the Viennese people should come to hear me, I would be able to please them with the music they liked best.

Schubert was Vienna's own musician. During his lifetime his fellow citizens had not been careful even to feed and lodge him, and he was invited only once — that was in his last year — to conduct a concert from the bulging portfolios of his works. He died at thirty-one of typhus fever, a disease which flourishes in filth and poverty. Yet now that he had been dead nearly a hundred years, the city was proud of him and jealous for the interpretation of his songs.

I Take Last Leave of My Mother

I had a good many of the six hundred songs of Schubert in my repertoire at that time: the Shakespearean lyrics, "Hark! Hark! The Lark" and "Who is Sylvia?" for which he made settings in a single afternoon, the first at a tavern in the midst of his daily walk and the other upon his return; the *"Erlkönig,"* from the composer's nineteenth year; the first half of Opus 89, the *"Winterreise"* — Schubert wrote six of the twenty-four songs in one morning — and Opus 23, the *"Schwanengesang,"* of which six of the songs were taken from Heine's *Buch der Lieder*. I like the Schubert music for the quality which suggests improvisation and spontaneity, and for its highly colored, imaginative feeling. It lends itself to emotional re-creation and can be made to sound endlessly fresh and inspired.

Robert Schumann was not a true Viennese and he was inclined to be contemptuous of Schubert — he said that Schubert would have been willing to set the words of an advertising handbill to music — but the people of Vienna loved his romanticism. Attempting to outdo Schubert in all things, Schumann protested that he had begun to compose at the age of six, whereas his rival was thirteen when he wrote his first piece; and claimed to have written one hundred and fifty songs in the year 1840. That was the year of his elopement with Clara Wieck, who had been playing his music publicly since she was twelve years old. Until he was thirty, Schumann composed principally for the pianoforte, but the romantic delights and passionate tempests of his unequal married life seemed to require expression in songs.

I have always felt in Schumann's music a kind of nervous quality which, if it is actually inherent, probably reflects his habitually overwrought nervous condition. When he was about thirty-four years old, he began to complain of mental exhaustion. Whenever he sat down to compose he was seized with paroxysms, and the note A sounded continuously in his ears. He tried to commit suicide by throwing himself into the Rhine, and finally died in a madhouse. Amongst the *Lieder* of his great year, 1840, and the immediately succeeding years, were the lovely lyric, "*Im Wunderschönen Monat Mai,*" and the sixteen songs of the "*Dichterliebe*" (Opus 48). I sang the Heine poem, "*Ich hab im Traum geweinet,*" that year in Vienna, and put it in my program for the American tour the following year.

The *Wiener Mittags-Zeitung* ran a story about me — that was in April, 1923 — under the caption, "A Black Lord of Song." I was described as "a small, agile Negro with crisp hair, thick lips and shining white teeth," but it was intimated that my exotic appearance had not spoiled my singing. One writer pleased me by saying that "no German could sing Schubert with more serious or unselfish surrender." Another was reminded of Lord Byron's exclamation — the poetry of Byron had fed the romantic imagination of more than one German song-writer — "Are not the hills, the waves, the sky, all part of myself and my soul, as I am a part of them?" But of all the critical notices, I think the one that pleased me most was an account in the *Wiener Allgemeine Zeitung:* "Do not imagine," the reviewer admonished his readers, "that it is sufficient to be white to become an artist; try first to sing as well as this black man did."

It was probably that comment which inspired an entry which I made in my fragmentary journal in Paris, the following June. "Although I know my face to be black," I wrote, "I am persuaded that the Spirit's choice of my body to inhabit has some specific purpose. . . . I am not pleased when I am told that my being black does not 'matter.' It does matter, it very much matters. I am black for some high purpose in the mind of the Spirit. I must work that purpose out."

I returned to England and Wales to keep a number of summer engagements at fifty guineas each, and then, armed with letters of introduction from friends in Paris, I went back to Vienna to settle down and study. I was determined to establish myself throughout Austria and Germany as a singer in the great *Lieder* tradition. My reputation in Paris was now reasonably secure: I had sung there in June to overflowing audiences, and Paul Landormy had wondered, in *La Victoire*, whether Paris had a single tenor who knew his *métier* as well as I. "Do not take M. Hayes for a savage," he had written. "He could give points to the most refined musicians in our own civilization, in the way of spinning sound from the starting point of the melody to its finality." I liked the figure about spinning out the sound, because to me the essence of singing is the perpetuation of the vocal line. And in fact, I liked everything about Paris and wanted to live there, to move and have my being in that unambiguous air. I only wanted first to try my luck in German.

I went to Dr. Theodore Lierhammer for coaching in the Viennese tradition, through the early fall of 1923, and on the evening of September 26, I was scheduled to give my second concert, under the auspices of an agency in which Anni Schnitzler, a niece of Arthur Schnitzler, was a partner. I was sure I now had the technical capacity for singing *Lieder*, and I had every reason to believe that my program was impeccable. Nevertheless, I woke up that day feeling heavy-hearted.

I confessed my depression to Dr. Alain Locke, who was visiting me at my hotel in the Ring. We were old friends and his mother was devoted to mine. I said that I was overcome with weariness and fatigue. He urged me to pull myself together, reminding me that I would be in competition with Jeritza, who was making one of her perennial farewell appearances at the Opera that night. But again in the evening, on the way to the concert hall with Dr. Lierhammer, I thought I could not possibly force myself to sing. I felt as though my heart were frozen. Lierhammer only said that I was bound to keep my engagement — as of course I knew I must.

I opened my program, as my custom was, with songs of the seventeenth and eighteenth centuries, went on to Schubert, Wolf, and Brahms, and concluded with a group of spirituals. But all the while it seemed to me that I was outside of my music, approaching it indifferently. I sang my way through the evening so introspectively that I was not aware of any response from my audience. After the concert I was broken-hearted, I thought I had failed. Anni Schnitzler came into the Green Room and found me weeping.

"Dear Roland," she said, "why do you look so unhappy? Are you exhausted? I have never heard you sing with such feeling. What new fire has been lighted so deep inside your body?"

"Don't speak to me," said I, "I know it was terrible." And I burst into tears again upon her shoulder.

Anni dried my eyes and made me speak to the people

who had come to see me. I shook hundreds of hands, but I could not bring myself to speak to anybody. Dr. Lierhammer came in with Simeon Rumschiski, the orchestra director, who had been my great friend in London. Rumschiski took me in his arms and said, "My poor Roland, my poor Roland." I was desolate. I broke down completely. I could not bear to think he had heard me sing badly.

Then he said, "Roland, I have something to tell you. I'm afraid your mother is very ill."

"She is dead," I said. I knew it in my bones.

"Yes," said Simeon, "your mother is dead."

I was crushed. My body ached irremediably in every nerve and fiber. I felt I must ease it by walking, and hurried off to my hotel alone. I went up to my room, and there loneliness closed in around me. All night I bruised and then comforted myself with the repetition of my mother's well-remembered words. In the morning I found I could face the world again because I was able to hear in my heart the last word she had spoken to me, not many months past: "Son," she had said, "you are the continuation of me."

Throughout the summer I had received frequent letters from her, and I read them over and over during the sad days that followed. Ma had been worried about my spiritual condition and her letters were full of Scrip-

tural admonition. She had taken to heart the hard saying of Jesus: "There is no man that hath left house, or
brethren, or sisters, or father, or mother, or wife, or
children, or lands, for my sake, and the gospel's, but
he shall receive an hundredfold now in this time, houses,
and brethren, and sisters, and mothers, and children,
and lands, with persecutions; and in the world to come
eternal life." This, like everything else the Bible said,
Ma thought, was right. All else was wrong. She wanted
me to be right in the Lord's way, not rich or great in
my own.

There was also much practical advice in those letters.
"Don't let praise make you kill yourself," she wrote.
"Don't sing yourself out." Again, speaking of a friend
of ours, a man in his thirties who had just married a girl
of seventeen, Ma said she hoped I would marry a
woman who had reached her twenties. "She will have
a grown mind," she observed. On the other hand —
Ma could be explicit — she did not want me to "marrie
an old woman for money."

Ma was still worried about my brother Robert, who
had lately suffered the withering of an arm, a catastrophe
all the more cruel because he had spent years in training to become my accompanist and had lately achieved
the required musicianship. He had planned to join me
in the winter of 1923, at the latest, and now all his

labor was lost. Ma thought he ought to go out and get a "one-handed man's job," in order to save himself, and prove himself a man. She liked men to be men.

What with her cares and the advancing years, Ma was "nearly wore out, both inside and outside," and she wrote in midsummer that she was ready to die — if only she could be sure that her sons trusted with her in the Lord.

In her last letter Ma told me that she was leaving her personal things to me, although she wanted the farm to go to the three of us, Jesse and Brantie and me. The letter closes on a characteristic note: "Well, Roland, stay in the bounds of reason. Do not let the folks cheer you to death. Watch yourself. I don't think you have as much flesh on you as you had when you let the Lord do for you. Watch how you use the fisical man. Don't worry about me. I'm alright. I have the whole Church around me."

The "whole Church" was still around her at her funeral. A great procession, two blocks long, walked behind her coffin along the way from the church to the cemetery. I cabled to the minister and asked him to play at the service my recording of the spiritual, "You're Tired, Chile, So Sit Down." Ma used to sing it in the Flatwoods, and over her ironing board in Boston. I sang it to the King and Queen of England in Buckingham

Palace, and made a record of it for my mother only a little while before she died. Somehow it lightened my grief a little, to think of her at rest.

I was too far away to go home to bury my mother. Instead, I took hold of myself and went on with my concerts. That was my duty, as Ma would have been the first to tell me. I made a fall season in Graz and Budapest, Karlsbad, and Prague, and in the last of these cities I encountered a brand-new experience. Elsewhere I had excited curiosity, even hostility, by merely being a Negro, but in Prague I was denounced as pro-German!

Because the *Lieder* were now indispensably a part of my repertoire, I had been booked in the only concert hall in which the German language could be used there. I had announced a program beginning with Italian songs, Scarlatti, Galuppi — the *"Evviva Rosa Bella,"* which I had copied out from a British Museum manuscript — and Mozart; continuing with Schubert, Brahms, and French and English composers; and concluding with Negro spirituals. At the last minute I wanted to make a change in the program order, but none of my staff could make an announcement in the Czech language. I was obliged to ask my accompanist, Leo Rosenek, to go out and tell the audience in German what I proposed to do. Rosenek had hardly opened his mouth when the mayor of Prague, who had lately taken office on an anti-German platform, raced up to the stage to harangue the people in their own language. All over the hall men and women rose to their feet. They milled about in the aisles, waving their arms and shouting imprecations. I entered from the artists' room, where I had been keeping an eye on the auditorium, and quietly took my place beside the piano, half expecting to be mobbed.

At length the mayor turned to me and said, in English, "Mr. Hayes, this concert cannot go on until you apologize to the people of this city for speaking in the German language. It is forbidden here."

"Sir," I replied, "I have paid for the right to *sing* in German in this place. I did not suppose that a well-intentioned speech in that language would give offense. If it was offensive, I am sorry. And now may I say that I think you owe me an apology for having interrupted my concert."

I was angry and the mayor was enraged. Rosenek advised a retreat, but the Germans in the audience clamored for their rights. I asked the mayor if he would be so good as to withdraw from the hall and permit me to fulfill my licensed engagement. Such an uproar ensued amongst the Czechs that I returned to the artists' room and made preparations to seek the safety of my hotel.

I Take Last Leave of My Mother

In a moment a Czech lady entered and introduced herself to me in English. She made a formal apology in the name of the citizens of Prague, explained that the new local government was fiercely nationalistic — as indeed the whole newly autonomized State had a natural right to be — and asked me to wait while she spoke to the audience. Rosenek and I returned to the concert platform with her. Leo sat down at the piano and I stood by.

The mayor charged about in his seat like an angry bull while the lady was speaking. First I tried to stare him out of countenance. Then I smiled at him, and he appeared to relax a little. Finally I beckoned him to join us on the stage.

"I think we have misunderstood each other," I said. "Let's shake hands."

His Honor consented to be appeased and I went on with the concert. As if to make atonement for the unpleasantness I had been exposed to, the audience rushed up to the platform, after my last encore, picked me up bodily, carried me around the courtyard and out to my automobile. Two hours earlier I had barely escaped being torn apart as the villain, now I was in danger of my life as the hero of the piece.

The next time I went to Prague, I temporized with the *Lieder* and sang in a Czech concert hall, Smetana

Salle. The manager called upon me the day before the concert to propose that I learn a word or two of the Czech language. I could so easily have the people of Prague at my feet, he said, and handed me an excerpt from "The Bartered Bride."

I protested that I did not see how I could learn a new aria in a strange language overnight.

"Sing my poetic English translation, down to the last line," he said, "and give us the last few words in Czech. I can teach you that much in five minutes."

Now I have always been able to make handy additions to my repertoire. The technique of song is fixed in my nature and I have acquired knowledge of the various schools. When I am confronted with a new song I have simply to put two and two together. I learn the text and sing it according to natural and acquired patterns: just s in my childhood I used to go out in the woods with ay friends to pick wild muscadine, on a Monday morning, and sing them the whole of yesterday's sermon, automatically acting in obedience to my nature.

So, at the end of the third group of songs the next evening, I was able to enter, by way of encore, upon the love theme from "The Bartered Bride." When Rosenek struck the first notes of the accompaniment the people rose from their seats. I sang through the English text, of which I now remember nothing, and then came upon

(*180*)

the single Czech line. The phonetic version, as it was written out for me, went something like this: *"Laska, laska o-ze-gni"* — which apparently meant "Love, love only." At the first *Laska* the emotions of the audience spilled out all over the hall; and while the rest of the line came out in a climax of warm, high notes, men and women tossed their hats and furs up into the air as though they had been in a *plaza de toro* in Madrid or Mexico City. After that, I felt no need for the protectorship which my Viennese manager had solicitated for me from the American Legation in Prague: a request which a *chargé d'affaires ad interim* had sharply rejected in three paragraphs of thorny longhand.

Late in the autumn of 1923, after my first visit to Prague, I went home to make the first of seven prolonged transcontinental tours. Robert had packed up the possessions Ma wanted me to have, together with the letters and papers she had accumulated, and closed up the little apartment I had shared with her in Roxbury. At the bottom of her travel-stained trunk, I found her last will and testament. It was written on a letterhead that had been printed for me when I was managing my own concerts, and dated at No. 3 Warwick Street, where we lived. This is the will, as Ma wrote it: —

I, Fannie Hayes, is writing my will. When I die I have 4 boys. I have 10 acres of land in Georgia. I want

(*181*)

my boys to have it and do what they like with it. I have a dollar or two in a bank here in Boston. At my death if I don't spend it before I die I want my boys to divide the money amoung themselves. Now my personal things, I have 3 quilts for the baby, one silk quilt, two cotton ones. If I stay with Roland till I die, all the other things I have is Rolands. He can do as he likes with them. This is Fannie Hayes will writen 13 day of April, 1916.

CHAPTER SEVEN

I Make My Bow to White America

M Y RECOLLECTIONS of my first official American tour are largely onomastic. I visited all of the places mentioned in Walt Whitman's poem, "Starting from Paumanok," and a great many more: —

> Americanos! conquerors! marches humanitarian!
> Foremost! century marches! Libertad! masses!
> For you a programme of chants.
> Chants of the prairies,
> Chants of the long-running Mississippi, and down to
> the Mexican sea,
> Chants of Ohio, Indiana, Illinois, Iowa, Wisconsin and
> Minnesota,
> Chants going forth from the centre from Kansas, and
> thence equidistant,
> Shooting in pulses of fire ceaseless to vivify all.

Whitman might have made something like this of my own list of names: —

Angel Mo' and Her Son, Roland Hayes

Bow to New England,
Haverhill, Springfield, New Bedford, New Haven,
    Providence, Worcester!
Sing to the Southland, Lexington, Louisville!
Out to far-spanning mid-distances,
Buffalo, Cincinnati and Pittsburgh! Chicago, Mil-
    waukee!
Songs for the sons of explorers,
Denver, Portland, Tacoma, St. Francis, City of An-
    gels! . . .

I wish I could report that the actuality was equally romantic. I sang three or four times a week, went to bed almost every night in a sleeping car, woke up in one or another of thirty strange cities, met delightful people whom I had no time to talk to, and worked desperately to keep my audiences interested and my body fit.

I was under professional management, at last, now that news of my success in Europe had reached my native shores, and my managers were reasonable gentlemen who gave me a degree of freedom not altogether common in those days. For example, I wanted to make my own programs. If such a wish seems natural and obvious, I can tell you that it is not often indulged, for concert agents almost invariably pretend to esoteric and infallible knowledge of the behavior of the public pulse. I asked to be relieved of the necessity of having my performances dressed up like a circus, with flood-lights and spotlights; and I liked having the texts of my songs printed on my programs, so that nobody could say, as my mother used to, "What was that you said, Roland?"

Before the tour began I appeared as soloist with the Boston Symphony Orchestra, under the direction of Pierre Monteux. I sang an aria from the ironical parody, *"Così fan Tutte,"* a work which Mozart presented to Francis I of Austria in return for an invitation to stay in Vienna and starve; and something from an oratorical trilogy, *"L'Enfance du Christ,"* by Hector Berlioz, the Holy Ghost of Théophile Gautier's "Trinity of Romantic Art." Philip Hale wrote a note about me for the program, so that I was able to make my debut *à la mode.* Only one circumstance marred the perfection of the evening. Not many of my own people were able to hear me. "Rush" seats were not easily available at subscription performances in Symphony Hall in those days.

It was thrilling to sing with that great choir of instruments. It used to tire me, when I was a boy in Chattanooga, to listen to symphonic compositions. I did not have the sensibility which necessarily accompanies the ear and translates, so to speak, the part each voice contributes to the performance of the whole. At Fisk I tried hard to learn to hear ensemble music, to follow it line

upon line, now this voice and now that, until my ear
could pick up color, clear and distinct and not blurred.
First I played recordings of Schubert quartets, and
learned to follow the development of themes. Then I
plunged into Beethoven. I was almost beside myself with
excitement when I found that my ear could catch the-
matic progressions from violin to 'cello, to English
horn or oboe, and separate threads of discourse from
their harmonic background.

During my student days in Boston, as soon as I could
afford it, I went on Saturday nights to the Symphony,
which was then conducted by Dr. Karl Muck, and there
I came to experience the peculiar evocations of symphonic music. Kreisler came one time to play a Bach
concerto, and the *adagio* movement, which is played
mostly on the G string, carried me away from this
earth. My heart was still full of that experience many
years later, when I went to hear the same great artist
play the same Bach music at the Opera in Paris.

Bach used to be, for me, the most difficult of composers to listen to, and when I had trained myself to
hear his music with the whole man, I was satisfied that
I had become a musician myself. The study of counter-
point taught me to think of the melody of a song and its
background as one piece of musical material, and to
use my voice as though it were an instrument: as though

(*186*)

I Make My Bow to White America

I were bowing a violin, for example, and intent, like the violinist, upon keeping melodic line and phrasing intact, while aiming at a high peak of virtuosity in the *ensemble*.

I remember an interesting comment that Dr. Lierhammer made when I sang *"Bist du bei Mir"* and "Steal Away" for him in Vienna. He said he was surprised to find how much the Negro spirituals and the music of Bach had in common. Both seemed to him to call for the same treatment of vocal line, the same religious approach. Even the rhythms of Bach and the spirituals are similar: for example, the motion is constant, even in sostenuto passages. Dr. Lierhammer thought I should be able to sing Bach naturally because I had inherited the capacity to feel religious joy. I made my first American essay at singing the work of that composer on the occasion of my debut in New York, a few days after the concert in Boston.

My Cousin Alzada came into the Green Room to see me, after my Town Hall debut, and thereafter she was the light of my eye. She looked like a little princess. She was in a sleeveless dress with bodice and basque of pale-pink velvet. A row of black buttons ran down the back of her waist and two or three pink bands encircled the hem of her black-satin skirt. She wore patent-leather pumps and a black satin turban trimmed with ermine tails, which dipped and curtsied behind her ears. She was working as an expert seamstress at the Stork Infants' and Children's Clothing Store, and had made those wonderful clothes herself. She brought me a beautiful cake of her own baking, and a pot of raspberry jam. Before I knew it I was in love with her, and impatient for engagements that would take me back to New York.

The morning after the concert I dearly wished that my mother had been with me, so that I could show her the papers. She would have taken pleasure in Heywood Broun's column about me in the *New York World*.

"Roland Hayes sang of Jesus," said Mr. Broun, "and it seemed to me that this was what religion ought to be, it was a mood rather than a creed, an emotion rather than a doctrine. There was nothing to define and nothing to argue about, each person took what he wanted and felt what he wanted to feel and so there was no heresy. . . . I saw a miracle in Town Hall. Half of the people were black and half were white and while the mood of the song held, they were all the same. They shared together the close silence. One emotion wrapped them. And at the end it was a single sob."

Before my time, white singers had too often been in the habit of burlesquing the spirituals with rolling eyes

(*188*)

and heaving breast and shuffling feet, on the blasphe-
mous assumption that they were singing comic songs.
It pleased me to believe that I was restoring the music
of my race to the serious atmosphere of its origin, and
helping to redeem it for the national culture.

The following night I sang a concert of my own in
Symphony Hall, in Boston, and received a substantial
part of the box-office receipts of nearly five thousand
dollars. This was the greatest amount of money I had
received for a single evening up to that time — twelve
thousand dollars was my all-time high — and my management was inspired to book me for two more recitals
there that season. For several years following I was one
of a small group of three or four artists — I believe I
am right in saying this — who could fill both Carnegie
Hall and Symphony Hall three times every winter.

When I reached my dressing room on the afternoon
of the third Boston concert — it was February 3, 1924
— I heard that Woodrow Wilson had just died in his
sleep. I had come to appreciate that great man during
my residence in Europe, where his statesmanship was
perhaps more generally regarded than at home, and
I wanted to pay some tribute to him. I walked up to
the front of the concert platform, after my entrance,
and held up my hand for silence.

"I have just learned of the death of a great soul," I

said, "and I am going to sing something for a memorial
to him." I sang "Goin' Home," with a theme from the
"New World Symphony," in an arrangement by William Arms Fisher: —

> Goin' home, goin' home, I'm jes' goin' home;
> It's not far, jes' close by, through an open door.
> Work all done, care laid by,
> Gwine to fear no more.

I think we were all moved by the plain melody and
simple sentiment of that homely spiritual, and after I
had sung it we were quiet for a long time.

My managers dispatched several cargoes of *feuilletons* to the South, describing my first Boston and New
York concerts, and I followed on a long tour in their
wake. In Birmingham, a municipal ordinance was specially promulgated to allow white people and Negroes
to sit under one roof, although nothing was said of the
remaining problem of persuading the legally mixed audience to sit together. It was sensibly agreed, at length,
that the race which bought the most tickets should
have the most seats. Three thousand Negroes bought
tickets and filled up the floor. The white people sat in
the balcony. The staff of the *News* at Fisk University
devoted a whole issue to me, white newspapers everywhere printed my picture, and more than one editor
hoped that the whole population would turn out when

I Make My Bow to White America

I came again. Only Atlanta, the capital of my home state, refused to hear me at that time. The Boston office had written a letter about me to an Atlanta manager and received a reply in basic English — "Atlanta isn't interested in niggers."

From the South, we swung out towards the West, and in Indianapolis, a bit of the past caught up with me. During one of the intermissions in my recital there, an usher handed me an envelope addressed to "Professor Rowland Hayes." It contained a Christmas card from the Reverend G. William Ward, the preacher who baptized me in the Tennessee River when I was fifteen years old. I invited him to come and see me in the artists' room after the concert, we talked over old times, and the next day he wrote me a letter. He congratulated me on having reached "the *Road* to *Fame*." He thanked God that he had taken some part in my religious life, and hoped that I would make a practical demonstration of my religion by sharing my income: for he supposed that I had more money than I needed.

For himself, said the Reverend Mr. Ward, he felt he was beyond the reach of help, except as the Lord was willing to provide. He had lately lost a matter of six hundred dollars in a real-estate deal, a thousand dollars in a rubber factory, and pickpockets, he said, had "hit" him for four hundred dollars and a diamond ring. Furthermore, there was an overdue mortgage of fifteen hundred dollars on his house. He would count it a blessing if I could make up those sums until the Lord got around to providing. I calculated I had bought my baptism dear.

I always enjoyed my visits to the Pacific Coast, where, on one occasion, managerial pride led to the hiring of the Civic Auditorium in San Francisco, a kind of Roman arena which seats some twenty thousand people. I stood on a little deck in the center of the circle — an enclosure which had seen more of prize-fighters than of singers — and looked out into an infinity of space. The farthest reaches of my audience were so remote that I knew the distant auditors had heard me only when I saw the faint flutter of their programs, and I was so far away from the uppermost benches that all the people up there could see of me was my teeth and the whites of my eyes. A few days later, in Santa Barbara, I learned a rule of life from a musician who had got it from his Russian violin teacher: "Don't work too soon, don't work too fast, don't work too long."

I returned from the West to round out that season with a third concert at Carnegie Hall in New York, and on the following day I received the most extraordinary letter. "Dear Mr. Hayes," my not very coherent correspondent began, "I want to apologize for having behaved like a cat."

I Make My Bow to White America

I called up a friend at the box office and asked him if he knew anything about the writer of that letter. He told me that a Southern woman had come to him a day or two before the concert to protest against my appearance in Carnegie Hall. She seemed to be determined to hear me, however — my friend said he did not quite understand why — and she was furious because she could not buy a ticket at the last moment. She was informed that a dollar and a half would buy her the privilege of standing up at the back of the hall. That was the only alternative to missing the concert.

"I wouldn't pay a dollar and a half to *sit down* and hear a nigger," the lady said, but pay she evidently did, because after the recital she looked up my friend and told him that she had changed her mind about me.

"I stood behind the railing," she said, "and waited for the monster to come in. When he came out on the platform, I turned my back. I couldn't bear to look at him. It made me mad to see him standing there" — she must have taken a peek at me — "with his head bowed and his eyes closed and his hands folded." It appears that she had expected me to begin with some cacophonous blast, and the soft, lovely entry of Handel's "A Tender Creature" disarmed her, broke her down. Her conscience would not let her rest until she had made her *mea culpa* to my friend and me.

Angel Mo' and Her Son, Roland Hayes

I suppose I was more sensitive to public and critical opinion at that time than at any other period of my life, because I was subjected then to the severest test of my career. Leipzig and Vienna, the most fastidious cities in the world, had liked me well enough, but now I was come to judgment in my own country. Success at home was of greatest moment to me. Ever since the color of my voice had been revealed to me, I had given myself wholly and deliberately to being, above all, a Negro artist, and I needed now either public approval or redirection. That is why it meant so much to me to read in Detroit, where I sang with the Symphony Orchestra, that I had made the spirituals sound "almost as though they had been written by a great master." A Chicago critic thought — although he felt it required orientation to look at a black man singing *"Die Forelle"* — that the personal and racial quality of my voice added something of value to the music of white men. Thus was my object little by little advanced.

Whenever a Negro has risen to an eminent position in any of the public activities of mankind, it has invariably been said of him, at one time or another, that he must have had a white ancestor somewhere along the line. There is no drop of white blood in my veins, hence there is no trace of it in my face or figure, as

I Make My Bow to White America

another Chicago critic once observed in the *Evening Post*. My voice could not be explained by inheritance under the rose from some Georgia Squire, therefore it had to be appraised for what it obviously was. The critical world may have found me perplexing, but it made the honorable confession that I had a new kind of vocal instrument, with its own individual color. If it was said of me merely that the color of my voice was good, I was ready to give myself to the restless and straining and fatiguing life of the concert halls.

I must say that my country was more than generous to me on that first tour, and in more ways than one. In Europe it used to be said that the artist's reward was immaterial. Foreigners and Americans alike appeared in Continental concert halls for *cachets* hardly more impressive than the wages of ushers and box-office attendants. Our European managers taught us to look to America for the translation of *succès d'estime* into box-office success, and apparently I was an apt pupil. After I had paid every penny of an appalling schedule of expenses, I still had ten thousand dollars to put in the bank at the end of my tour. I had saved all that money in spite of the fact that I had nearly always been required to pay — as indeed I still do — at least fifty per cent more than white artists are charged for hotel accommodations and services. Furthermore, my professional career was well launched at home, along with the bull market of the twenties.

II

During the summer of 1924 I received the Spingarn Medal. No prouder reward had come to me since April, 1922, when, in the presence of Miss Robinson, Dr. Thomas Jesse Jones gave me the degree of Doctor of Music at Fisk University, the first honorary degree ever conferred by my Alma Mater. Theodore Roosevelt, Dorothy Canfield Fisher, and W.E.B. Du Bois were members of the committee which made the Spingarn award in my year, and Dr. Joseph H. Penniman, President of the University of Pennsylvania, handed the Medal to Harry Burleigh as my representative. I was unable to be present because I was solidly booked up abroad through the summer season. In fact, on the very evening of the presentation, I was singing again before the Queen of England in Lady Harcourt's house in Mayfair.

A year later, just before I sailed from New York aboard the *Aquitania*, Dr. Walter Damrosch presided at a little ceremony up on deck, and I officially became the tenth Spingarn Medalist. James Weldon Johnson, the secretary of the National Association for the Advancement of Colored People, called upon Dr. Damrosch to make a speech. I did not have very much to say in reply. My heart and my throat were too full, and my mind overflowed with images of the "dark hours" through which my great-grandfather, my grandfather, and my mother had passed in order to produce the music which I was destined to sing. I went back to my stateroom and placed the new trophy in my treasure box, along with the diamond stickpin which King George and Queen Mary had given me.

Before the end of the season in London, in the summer of 1924, my Boston manager wrote to me to say that I would have to prepare three separate programs for my next American tour. He had booked me again to appear three times in Boston, and in New York as well. I went straight to Prague, to join the only friend I had in the world who could help me in such an ambitious undertaking. After the death of my mother, the Countess Hoyos of Vienna had written to a friend of hers, a highborn lady who lived in a château near the Czech capital, to ask her to look out for me during my first visit there. The lady from Prague, the daughter of a nobleman and the mother of a boy who was heir to a historical title, became my indispensable friend. She responded to the Countess Hoyos's warm appeal by calling on me at my hotel. She introduced herself charmingly, as though she were asking instead of conferring a favor.

"The Countess Hoyos has most kindly made it possible for me to meet you," she said. "My friends and I are delighted when we can come to know the visiting artists. It helps us to enter into their art."

I told her a good deal about myself — in fact, I am afraid I poured out most of the story of my life into her sympathetic ears — and then I described the program I was to sing in Prague.

"With what added pleasure my friends and I now shall be able to listen to you," the aristocratic lady said, and took her leave of me in the gilded *salon* where we had been sitting.

To that lady and her son and all her numerous and powerful clan I owe the real beginning of my intellectual life and my musical maturity. In their company I learned to sing with authority. I was able to consult in their houses all of the vocal masterworks of all the great composers. I sang from the seven volumes of Schubert with my friend, and that was only the beginning of my education. In preparation for my visits she would assemble a bibliography of whatever composer we had nominated for study. We read the definitive biographies and sang and played the music in chronological sequence. In such a way, year after year, we went through Bach, Handel and Mozart, Schubert and Schumann, Beethoven, Brahms and Hugo Wolf, and then the early Italian masters. We read Goethe, Schiller, and Bismarck for background. Whenever I appeared, from America or England, from Paris or Germany, my friend would be waiting to plunge with me into new problems, with shelves of books and stacks of music ready for research and study. Thus, when I had occasion to sing a song of this or that composer, I was able to put the sum of his works into my interpretation of a single piece. Sometimes, indeed, I have felt that I have drawn directly upon the resources of his whole school and epoch.

In the midst of a concert, a singer has only a fleeting moment in which to convey the musical culture of a composer's lifetime. How can he, in that moment, convey all that is to be said unless he has added up the whole sum of the composer's work? For example, when I sing one of the Schubert *Lieder*, I mean to bespeak attention to the overtones of the other five hundred and ninety-nine. And so many songs stem from instrumental scores — as *"Die Forelle"* is to be found embedded in the Trout Quintet — that the singer is often bound in conscience to project his music against an imaginary background of unheard flutes and violins and horns.

As tired as I was after an exacting tour at home or

on the Continent, I found it so exciting to spend long weeks working with my friend, during the late months of summer and early fall, that I was able each winter, from 1924 to 1930, to take up my work in America as fresh as a cucumber. And I must say that there were many times when I needed all the resources of energy and enthusiasm I could store up abroad.

In American cities which I visited for the first time, I often found the audiences inquisitive or skeptical, or even hostile. The Secretary of the American Missionary Association used to say, in a sermon which he was preaching up and down the country in 1924, that race prejudice was growing in the North and diminishing in the South. I could not see, when I was on my second American tour, that the old prejudices had been abated anywhere. My managers tried to spare me discomfort and humiliation by making traveling arrangements for me well in advance, but even so, hotelkeepers now and again refused to put me up when the day of my arrival actually rolled around. This happened to me in the West as well as in the East, in Tucson and Phoenix and in Washington and Baltimore. In Tucson, when rooms were denied me, I had only a few hours to rest after a sleepless night, and I was on the point of canceling my concert when a well-disposed white citizen came to me with the hospitable offer of lodging in his own house.

I Make My Bow to White America

A Jim-Crow scandal, not at all of my own making, was stirred up in the press all the way from Los Angeles to New York, but I am not sure that my way thereafter was any smoother.

I think it was on that second tour that a lady impresario — her name was Mrs. Green — booked me for a concert in Baltimore and one in Constitution Hall in Washington. Some Daughters of the American Revolution, residents of the capital city — the Negroes call them "Lily Whites" — prevailed upon Mrs. Green to announce that white and colored patrons would sit in separate sections of the auditorium. The Negro population protested the prospect of segregation, and Mrs. Green telephoned to Boston to ask me what to do. I said that I could not undertake to solve the problem for her, but at the same time, I wanted to be sure that some solution would have been reached before I left for the South. It was ultimately reported to me that black and white people were going to sit together in Washington, and the Negroes of Baltimore had agreed to take a block of seats by themselves.

When I arrived at the railway station in Baltimore, I was astonished to find a mob of shouting Negroes who looked as though they would tear me apart. They had heard that tickets had been sold in Washington on equal terms, and were inclined to blame me for the

Baltimore iniquity. Some friends conducted me in safety, although not without anxiety, to a barricaded chamber, and there I sat out the hour before my concert. The hall was packed with people who had good-naturedly accepted the conditions, but outside a crowd still milled about and kept the building practically in a state of siege. I said I could not sing in the midst of such confusion, and only the copious tears of Mrs. Green persuaded me to make my entrance. I stepped up to the front of the platform and made a speech.

"I may not be able to finish my program," I said, "and if I do not finish it, you will all know why." And therewith I opened my program with the "Crucifixion," for that was exactly how I felt.

It was just about that time that Miss Dorothy Thompson cabled a story from Berlin, in which she quoted the American singer, Mme. Charles Cahier, as saying that "America was hard soil" for musical genius. The trouble was, said Mme. Cahier, that the American people did not have to have music to live. Only amongst the Negroes, she thought, could music be said to be a spontaneous accompaniment to the ordinary circumstances of living. She had spoken particularly of me, Miss Thompson wrote, because she felt that I had begun to penetrate the hard wall of native indifference to music. I do not know whether she realized that there was a second and more formidable wall of color to bar my way; and that, unlike Christian, I had no Evangelist at hand to direct me to a wicket gate whereby I might pass through it.

I suppose that in the long run I sang with most of the illustrious orchestras of those days — for music, like money, eventually breaks artificial barriers down. When Koussevitzky took the Boston Symphony Orchestra to New York in January, 1925, I was the tenor Narrator in Berlioz's "Repose of the Holy Family." People made fun of Dr. Koussevitzky's extravagance in bringing eight women from Boston to sing ten angelic measures at the end of the Berlioz aria, but the great perfectionist was unperturbed. In the same season I sang a group of spirituals at a New York Philharmonic concert under Bruno Walter, and during the following season Stokowski gave me about the most satisfying orchestral accompaniment I ever had. That was in Philadelphia, at the Academy. Stokowski permitted me to name my own music, and I chose the Mozart aria, "*Si mostra la sorte*," and three spirituals which Rosenek had orchestrated for me. I fared well under those famous hands.

The name of an American composer, Charles Tomlinson Griffes, began to appear on my programs of that year, along with Handel and Schubert, Ravel and De-

Angel Mo' and Her Son, Roland Hayes

bussy. When I first saw the Griffes songs in Paris, a few years after the composer's death in 1920, I thought they were fascinating, for they were personal and colorful — and withal extremely difficult. Griffes, who had lived for a time in the Orient, had learned to think of music in Oriental fashion. He found the Oriental ear so delicately trained that it could readily follow an instrumental line through a maze of voices, and in much of his own music the accompaniment exhibits that kind of detachment from the vocal line of the song. I used to sing two Griffes songs frequently: "In a Myrtle Shade," from William Blake's *Ideas of Good and Evil:* —

> O how weak and weary I
> Underneath my myrtle lie!

and "Rose of the Night," from a poem by Fiona Macleod.

"There is an old mystical legend," wrote William Sharp, "that when a soul among the dead woos a soul among the living, so that both may be reborn as one, the sign is a dark rose, or a rose of flame, in the heart of the night." The poem begins: —

> The dark rose of thy mouth
> Draw nigher, draw nigher!
> Thy breath is the wind of the south,
> A wind of fire,
> The wind and the rose and darkness, O Rose of my Desire!

I Make My Bow to White America

The music of Griffes's songs seems to me invariably beautiful, and I have always defended it against a conviction of pretentiousness. But I must confess to introducing an element of incongruity into my study of their florid *fin de siècle* texts. I learned them in a dentist's chair in Vienna.

I also employed at home the songs of Charles Martin Tornov Loeffler, a composer of Alsatian birth who became first-desk violinist with the Boston Symphony Orchestra about the time I was born. He wrote a number of Irish fantasies for voice and orchestra, and a "Canticle of the Sun" for solo voice with chamber accompaniment. Another naturalized American whose songs I have liked is Nicholas Slonimsky. I used to sing "My Little Pool," whose silver melody is sustained by an accompaniment in which the right hand plays on white keys while the left hand plays on black.

At the end of my second American tour, there was a piece in one of the magazines about the color of my voice. Mr. Maynard Walker read the article and wrote to me from his offices in the editorial department of the *St. Louis Post-Dispatch*. The letter followed me to Europe and I have kept it ever since, along with letters from my mother, a clipping from the *New York Times* entitled "From Stove Moulder to $100,000 a Year," and a photograph of a portrait of Abraham Lincoln.

(*205*)

Angel Mo' and Her Son, Roland Hayes

The portrait had been inscribed in Washington, on the third of October, 1861, by Lincoln himself: "For Mrs. Lucy G. Speed, from whose pious hand I accepted the present of an Oxford Bible, twenty years ago," and the photograph which I have of it is autographed by Hallie Bishop Speed, who gave it to me. The treasured letter which thus lies side by side with the Great Emancipator and the Alger-book account of my career contains these lines (I have learned them by heart): —

I have been wondering if your native race is not after all closer to the heart of the universe and its secrets — if it is not really a step nearer to the Unknown than our white race. There are so many things that point that way, and one thing is your voice, and your attitude toward it — your whole attitude toward life, for that matter, and the strange, great, uncanny foreknowledge that seems to guide you in the same way that fish swim in the sea.

CHAPTER EIGHT

I Follow the Black Army to Germany and Washington Irving to Spain

I EARLY LEARNED in Europe that concert-hall managers are sometimes reluctant to pay for songs which have already been sung. No marketable commodity is more ephemeral than a concert of music: when it has been performed, it leaves no tangible residue for a court to restore to a defrauded manufacturer. Hence many of my elders were in the habit of protecting themselves by collecting their fees in advance of performance. Vexed managers used to expose this custom to the public for the purpose of creating ill will, so that if an artist, upon occasion, kept an audience waiting while a negligent entrepreneur delayed the payment of a contracted fee, he was likely to be blamed for being worldly. I decided, however, in considering my first offer to sing in Budapest, to risk my reputation rather than my purse. I said I would come when I saw the cash money, and the Budapest manager, who turned out to be a most complaisant gentleman, sent me a check in American dollars. I deposited it in my bank in Paris, entrained for the fantastic sister cities which lie opposite each other on the banks of a muddy and sluggish stream — not at all the beautiful blue Danube of the waltz — and after that, I demanded advance payment from strange managers as boldly as my more sophisticated colleagues.

The American Consul General in Czechoslovakia advised me not to go on to Germany, which was next on my European itinerary, until the Allied Army of Occupation was withdrawn. The Dawes Conference had opened a way to the settlement of French and British differences, but the Pact of Locarno was still some months off; and meanwhile the German people were feeling bitterly about the black colonial troops in the Rhineland. I refused to believe, however, that they would hold me, a private Negro citizen of the United States, responsible for the presence of French-speaking Africans, and so I settled down in Prague to prepare for German audiences by polishing up my studies of the *Lieder*.

It interested me to trace the gradual development of *Lieder* from the early folk music of the Germanic peoples. Bach, Haydn, and Beethoven — as well as Purcell in England — frequently approached the forms which Schubert at a later time defined. The classical composers usually treated their music geometrically, to be sure, but in some of the songs which seem to anticipate Schubert, there are moods, if not notations, derived from folk melodies: as in Bach's little song called "The Pipe."

Perhaps the best illustration I can think of to show, within the range of *Lieder*, the transition from Bach to Schubert is Schubert's *"Du bist die Ruh,"* compared to Bach's *"Bist du bei Mir."* The *"Bist du bei Mir,"* from the notebook of Anna Magdalene Wülken, the wife who gave Bach his nine sons, is classical in form and folkloric only in feeling; whereas *"Du bist die Ruh"* is a fusion of the classical and romantic forms. That is, there is romantic "form" as well as flavor in Schubert, who yet did not leave classicism entirely behind. It is perhaps this very subtlety in the Schubert songs that has made them inimitable; so that Strauss, for example, seems to me to be at best a diluted poet.

As with so many of the forms of art, the *Lieder* reached their highest perfection in the hands of their originators. Beginning with classical ideas, Schubert — and Schumann after him — produced romantic inventions in the service of atmosphere and mood. They reproduced melodically the emotions given off by the poems which they set to music, while Bach and Handel treated their texts, from whatever source, according to the mathematical style which is summed up in the whole work of Bach. There is undeniably deep feeling in the inventive works of those two masters, but the romantic imagination which clothes the *Lieder* demands a greater exercise of the singer's own imaginative qualities than the works of their predecessors do. Each re-creation of a song by Schubert or Schumann, by Brahms or Wolf, requires the immediate play of romantic fancy. Hence the *Lieder* singer must keep himself steeped in the music and the literature of that endearing period.

Early in the fall of 1924 I felt ready to meet the Germans on their own terms. Some friends I had made in Pilsen helped me to cross the border inconspicuously, and I went up at once to Berlin. I wanted to get the feel of the city for a couple of days before the concert which a Russian agent by the name of Borkon had booked me to sing at the Beethovensaal. On my breakfast tray, the morning after my arrival, I found a complimentary copy of an American newspaper published in the German capital. The editorial page contained an open letter which proved that the consul in Prague had been no alarmist. Addressed to the American Ambassador, and signed by an officer of one of the many nationalistic societies which flourished in postwar Germany, it called for the prevention of a certain calamity: namely, the concert of an American Negro who had come to Berlin to defile the names of German poets and composers; a Negro, the writer said, "who, at best, could only remind us of the cotton fields of Georgia." I sent the Ambassador tickets for a box, which he turned over to members of his staff, and on the evening of the concert the box was filled to overflowing.

When I entered the concert chamber at the Beethovensaal, I found myself standing in a flood of light; in front of me, a black-out audience sat unquietly. From the rear there rolled out a great volley of hisses, which seemed to me to fill the hall entirely. I was terribly apprehensive, but I took my place in the curve of the piano, closed my eyes, lifted my head into singing position, and stood still as a statue. I waited moment after moment, perhaps for five or ten minutes altogether, listening to the ebb and flow of antagonistic sound. I tried to match the determination of my adversaries with quiet invincibility, and after a time I seemed actually to impress them. No one came to my defense on this occasion, so far as I could hear, but presently the attack upon me petered out.

When silence came, as it absolutely did at length, the hall was more still than any I had ever sung in. It was so quiet that the hush began to hurt. I conveyed my readiness to my accompanist with the slightest movement of my lips, without turning my head or my body, and began to sing Schubert's *"Du bist die Ruh,"* which otherwise would have occurred later in the program. The entry to that song is almost as silent as silence itself. The German text, stealing out of my mouth in sustained pianissimo, seemed to win my hostile audience over.

In the Green Room, during the first intermission, I was warned that no singer had dared to use the French language in Berlin since the war, but I was determined to face my audience out with the French songs printed in my program. I returned to the platform and sang Debussy, Henri Duparc, and Massenet. I sang the "Dream Song" five times. The audience accepted that group so gallantly that I gave them more of their own music before I went on to the spirituals.

The first person to speak to me in the artists' room after the concert was an American boy who was studying music in Berlin. His face was as red as a beet and his eyes shone darkly.

"Goddamn it," he said, "put it there! This is the first time I have seen the Germans admit that good art can come out of America."

Before I left Berlin I signed a contract for another

recital the following month and came to a gentleman's agreement for a return engagement the next year, at a sum of money unheard of in musical circles in Europe. Herr Borkon wrote to me after the second concert to say that it had been more successful than the first, "if it is only possible"; but even so, when I went back the third time, in 1926, I had some difficulty in collecting the money he had agreed to pay me.

It was in the contract that I was to be paid eight hundred dollars on the morning of my first concert, and eight hundred more before the second of the pair. On the day of the first recital I sat over my breakfast in the sitting room of my apartment and waited for Borkon to come with the money. I heard nothing from him until after lunch, when he sent his secretary to tell me that he had not yet been able to get so much money in American currency. He promised to hand it to me in the evening. I went early with Leo Rosenek to the Philharmoniesaal, but Herr Borkon was not there. I heard a clock strike the hour of my concert. Five minutes passed. It was reported to me that the audience was growing restless, but I waited another ten minutes. Then Borkon flew in, flushed and panting.

"So? You keep the public waiting, do you?" he asked angrily.

I protested. "It is you who are keeping them waiting," I said. "I will give you five minutes to pay me my money. After that time I shall go back to my hotel."

A good many minutes passed and I returned to my rooms. Borkon told the audience, as a clergyman from Boston described the scene to me later, that I had refused to sing because I had not got my money. He spoke disparagingly of me, in order to get himself out of the scrape, but someone in the hall — the clergyman did not know who it was — rose up in my defense.

"Take him his money this minute and fetch him back," he said.

When Borkon handed me my fee, I returned to the hall and sang my program to an audience which was perfectly receptive, in spite of a three-hour wait.

The newspapers, the following morning, were naturally not undivided in their attention to me. One paper took both sides, balancing a flattering criticism with an editorial entitled "The Naughty Negro who would not sing until he heard the money ringing in the till." Another editor resented the importation of foreign artists in general and me in emphatic particular, but a third defended me in an article headed "The Negro tenor only asked for his rights."

I do not remember that elsewhere in Germany, except in Hamburg, the Negro issue came up. The critic of one of the Hamburg newspapers reported that I had inaugurated the new season "under the sign of black," but he went on to say that "color bleaches under the rays of art, and what remains is man."

From Berlin I went to Leipzig, whose seventeenth-century labyrinth I entered in the spirit of a Crusader on a pilgrimage to the Holy Land. Bach had come to this place from Köthen exactly two hundred years before my time. I visited his tomb in the Thomaskirche, and breathed the air of the quarter where he created his purest music — most of his religious music, in fact, and many of Anna's songs.

I was a little appalled, when I walked out onto the shallow platform of the Kleinegewandhaus in Leipzig, to find that the people who sat in the front row of stalls were scarcely an arm's length away from me. I saw that I should have to sing straight into their near, unsmiling faces — unsentimental and monocled faces which stretched up at me out of a white wall of starched linen. I had never been so frightened, not since my first rhetorical back in the Flatwoods: the time when a two-line poem made me sick. I felt faint at the prospect of singing under the cold scrutiny and into the fastidious ears of that unexpectant audience.

I opened my program with Bach's "Take Me to Thee for Thine Own." My auditors took pains not to show what they thought, about either me or the song. They listened with reserve and responded with silence. Nor did they, during the course of the evening, ever really loosen up. At the end of the concert, a few gentlemen politely sounded the brass tips of their walking sticks against the floor. The rest undemonstratively walked out.

Leipzig is the only city I have ever sung in where the Negro spirituals were received without any sign of relish. The musicologists who wrote essays for the newspapers there treated them as interesting and quaint phenomena from another world, but not at all as music. My agent, who had warned me that Leipzig would be difficult, tried to comfort me with a report on the attendance. He pointed out that a people which cared only for its local classics, and rarely listened to foreigners, had at least put in an appearance and had remained to the end. That was all I could expect in that rarefied atmosphere. My only other reward, beyond a small sum of money, was an invitation to come back and sing five Bach arias with the symphony orchestra, a few weeks later. And in return for that honor, I was called upon to buy the scores for the whole society.

II

I crossed over to America in the early winter of 1924, after the German season, to sing the eighty concerts of my second American tour; and in April, 1925, after much embarrassing correspondence, I returned to Europe to sing with the Royal Philharmonic Society of Madrid. It was I alone who had occasioned the embarrassment, through sheer ignorance of the royal dignity of that orchestra. When the director offered me an engagement to sing in the Spanish capital, I not only made extravagant demands in the way of fees, but also, to conform with my new policy, required advance payment in American dollars. Pablo Casals, who lent me his accompanist for my visit to Spain, explained to me too late that the Society was under the direct patronage of the King and Queen; and I was the more humiliated by the situation I had created when I further discovered that Queen Mary had recommended me to the interest of the Spanish royalties, through Alfonso Merry del Val, Ambassador Extraordinary and brother of the Cardinal.

In Madrid, for the first time in my life, I played at something unrelated to my work. I went to parties everywhere, with the most fashionable people in the city; although I must confess that frequently I felt like an ox in a parlor amongst them. My visits to bullfights were somewhat less formidable; in fact, I enjoyed the *corridas* immensely. I was particularly fascinated by the formal plotting of each episode in its fixed period of twenty minutes — the stately and tragic progression of events from beginning to end. Although I learned to understand the necessary order of the drama, which reaches a climax when the bull is killed, I used to feel that the sharpest impact came with the first encounter of the bull with the *torero*. The initial meeting of brute force with lively skill always left me breathless.

When the strength of the bull is spent and his neck begins to droop, it is easy to see who the victor will be; but when he trots into the arena, fresh and strong and challenging encounter, and charges the bullfighter's scarlet cape, there is a moment of uncertainty, of ominous foreboding, of which the emotional excitement seems to me never to be quite equaled again before the death of the bull. There is many an instant of dangerous beauty when the bullfighter passes the bull with cape and *muleta*, but it is at the first meeting, if at all, that the man must establish his superior valor and cunning. To me, at any rate, there is a dramatic and awful issue when, at the rendezvous, the wonder flashes across the mind, "Which will survive, the bull or the man?" Although I experienced momentary horror and distaste as well, I went regularly to the arena during the season and watched the rise to ascendance of new artists and the disgrace of old heroes, and came withal to some appreciation of the quality of that peculiarly Spanish art.

I visited Toledo, with a party of friends, and walked up and down the winding lanes El Greco trod; I sang in Barcelona, the guest of a rich merchant who invited two hundred people to spend the week end with him in the country; and upon my return to Madrid I gave several concerts of my own. But all that while, I could not bring myself to sing the Spanish music. I had learned some Spanish songs in Vienna, with Dr. Lierhammer, and I listened to folk music from every quarter of Spain during the summer festival in Madrid, but the peculiar linear and rhythmical quality of the music remained alien to me. The *Lieder* were forms which I had been able to cultivate for myself, so to speak, and to reproduce, but the Spanish music, especially the traditional *flamenco*, is so completely autochthonous that its perfect rendering is beyond the grasp of people not of that soil themselves. I felt that my attempts to sing it would be as false as those of white people who try to sing the Negro spirituals. In any case, I think the *madrileños* preferred to hear the kind of songs I could sing well. They seemed to like the religious music of my own land.

A Lady in Waiting informed me, during one of my recitals, that the Queen Mother wished me to sing to her in the Palace the next evening. The chamberlain called the following day to give me instruction in Bourbon-Habsburg etiquette, and presented me with a token from the Queen, a stickpin studded with diamonds and sapphires: the Queen Mother's monogram under a jeweled crown. I remembered how diffidently and with what mumbled words King George had handed me a similar gift, a scarf pin with GM picked out in diamonds.

Queen Christina, a Regent during the minority of her son, Alfonso XIII, was of Austrian royalty, the daughter of the Archduke Charles Ferdinand and the Archduchess Elizabeth of Austria. When her husband, to whom she had been married before the Bourbon restoration, was recalled to become head of the Spanish kingdom, she resolved to make Madrid a center of culture, like Vienna. At the time of my presentation she was nearly seventy years old and had been through a good deal: civil revolution, war with the United States, the ticklish neutrality of the first World War; and yet she was still bright and lively and full to the brim of musical feeling. She especially wanted to hear Bach, Schubert, and the Negro spirituals. I walked with her through the Palace gardens, after my program, while she reviewed the history of Spain and asked me to describe the remains of Spanish culture in Latin America.

I Follow the Black Army

That was before I went to Mexico, a journey I made some years later so that I could see for myself something of the extraordinary quality of that syncretistic Republic, and so I listened to the Queen instead. She had at the tip of her tongue the incredible story of the political conquest of millions of Indians by a handful of diminutive warriors — a story which becomes probable only in the light of its historical background. The native population of the New World was disunited, for example, and superstition made them fearful of the creatures, half men, half horse, who descended upon them. Yet some element of fantasy remains. It is easier to conquer a country than to impose a new culture upon it, as the modern world well knows. How was it that a few Spanish *Conquistadores* and their confessors were able to give their language and their religion, their art and architecture, to every part of New Spain within a generation? Our own country was scarcely in its log-cabin era when the Spanish culture of the Latin areas had already begun to decay, after a brilliant flowering.

Queen Christina, along with her son's countrymen generally, still hoped for the restoration of Spanish influence in the Spanish-speaking countries of the Americas. It seemed to me when I visited Mexico, just before the present war, that the hopes of the Spanish aristocrats were unlikely of fulfillment. In the nineteenth century, rich Mexicans lived in France and Italy, rather than in Spain, and married their daughters to French and Italian noblemen; and in this century the new ruling classes, who have given shelter to Republican refugees from the mother country, appeared to me to be entirely unsympathetic with Franco's — and Hitler's — aspirations in the Western Hemisphere.

I returned to Spain the following year and stayed six weeks in Barcelona. Señor don Eusebius Bertrand y Serra, of one of the great families of that city, gave a musical party for me, so that I might hear some Spanish music. The principal singer was the Señorita Conchita Badia y Aguisti, who was accompanied at the piano by the *maestro* Manuel de Falla, many of whose songs she sang. Falla, who collected folksongs from all parts of Spain and sponsored festivals for the performance of native music, also played some of his piano music for us, of which I liked particularly the "Four Spanish Pieces."

There were also some arias from Granados's opera, *Goyescas*, an enlargement of a piano suite based upon the paintings and tapestries of the Spanish painter, Goya. I remembered hearing about the first performance of the opera at the Metropolitan in New York in 1916. Señor Granados and the Señora undertook the dangerous wartime journey to America to hear it and were drowned on their return to Spain. Their steamer, the *S.S. Sussex*, was torpedoed by a German submarine.

I was enchanted when at length I found myself on the way south to Granada. I explored every nook and corner of the Alhambra, which my friends in Prague had prepared me to see by reading aloud from Washington Irving. That stronghold of the Moorish monarchs, which stands on a hilly terrace overlooking the city from the south, seemed to me to be almost exactly as Irving had pictured it. I saw the same ruined halls and courtyards, whose leafy decoration, commissioned by Yusef I in the fourteenth century, neither vandalism nor nineteenth-century reconstruction had quite yet effaced. A turreted wall enclosed the palace in a park of perhaps thirty acres of myrtle and rose and citrus, and a stream still flowed through emerald shrubbery — although I did not hear that gold was being sifted from its sands.

I found my own Mateo Ximenes in the person of a *gendarmo* who could speak French and who looked as though he could protect me in case the countryside was still infested with dangerous vagrants. I am sure that my policeman was, like Washington Irving's guide, a son of the Alhambra, although he wore, instead of Mateo's tattered garb, the resplendent uniform of his office.

We used to go daily through the narrow entrance by

which strangers enter the palace, and into the patio de los Arrayanes, to look at the marble-ringed and myrtle-bordered goldfish pool; or into the Court of Lions, with its alabaster reservoir; or into the Hall of the Two Sisters, with a fountain which played up to the cornices of a stalactite-vaulted roof. I rode mule-back into the hills and followed watercourses which fed the innumerable fountains. I made sketches everywhere, thinking to reproduce something of that aqueous beauty at my farm in Georgia, where springs bubble up out of the highest levels of Horn's Mountain.

I was in Granada in nightingale season, and lived in a little villa set into the very walls of the Alhambra. My rooms overlooked a magnolia grove where the nightingales sang. I was there in the month of May, and the birds, lately returned from Nubia and Abyssinia, sang both day and night. What a miracle of sound comes from the throats of those drab, inconspicuous creatures! It is only the cock that sings, to be sure, but he is no more elegant than his mate. He is a veritable Negro amongst birds, with his reddish-brown plumage — as anonymous in the magnolia glade as a colored boy in a field of cotton.

When my Mateo came to fetch me for our afternoon walks, he had to clear a place for me amongst the vagabonds who lined the sidewalk outside the doors of the villa, the maimed and the halt, beggars with running sores, and emaciated madonnas with hungry babies. These were the descendants of the "vagrants" of Washington Irving's day. Irving also spoke of "the caverns of the adjacent hills," which "swarmed with gipsies," and I inquired of my guide whether gypsies still lived in the near-by caves.

In my time there, in 1926, they appeared to have set up a kind of civil polity with which the city authorities seemed not to interfere. Dancing was their principal preoccupation, and their choreography suggested that the dances were really exercises of religion. Many of the so-called Spanish dancers I had seen in European music halls were excommunicates, so I was told, from those very tribes — disowned because they had gone out into a secular world. The Granada gypsies permitted themselves some degree of secularity at home, to be sure. They opened certain of their caverns to the paying public along about two o'clock every afternoon; and it was when Mateo informed me of this custom that I asked him to take me to visit them, along with the tourist throng. He protested that I should be received privately, as artist by artist, and he therefore arranged for an exclusive audience with the gypsy chief.

I was received at the entrance to the caves, the following morning, by an aide-de-camp who ushered me through a kind of maze in the honeycombed hillside. I was presented to the king in a small alcove hung with rugs and embroideries. He greeted me hospitably and clapped his hands. Twelve dancing girls came twinkling on their toes into a deep chamber which faced the alcove where I sat with the chief, and a matriarch of incredible age — I could not see the features of her face for the wrinkles — followed after to direct them. Each of the girls, beginning with the youngest, danced up and down the length of the earthen floor, executing first the traditional measures of *Jaleo de Jerez* or *Palotéa*, *Tirano* or *Tripola Trapola*, and then improvising on the basic steps of the *Fandango*. Their customary routine thus accomplished, they curtsied to the chief and disposed themselves along the walls of the room.

Amidst a flourish of castanets, guitars, and tambourines, the *primera bailarina* then entered in a whirl of color and danced the tribal version of the *Seguidilla*. Never have I heard or felt such rhythms: counter-rhythms, and anti-rhythms. The instruments seemed all to be played one against another, in violent antiphony; and as though the rhythmic disturbance so created were not sufficiently exciting of itself, the chorus along the wall produced another set of cadences by stamping their feet and clapping their hands.

Finally the grinning grandam herself, the grand-

I Follow the Black Army

mother of the *primera bailarina*, was persuaded to dance for me. Her supple limbs astonished me. Life seemed to flow once again over her old, dry bones. She accomplished the intricate patterns of a traditional dance with miraculous agility. She looked an ogreish old woman, a witch's head on a nimble body, and she seemed to epitomize the whole *flamenco* tradition in a cadaver. Still, I have never seen the art of dancing elsewhere so cunningly disclosed.

The *primera bailarina* came to me at the conclusion of the performance and said, "You are a musician, Señor."

"How do you know?" I asked.

"I see it in your eyes and in your hands, Señor," she replied.

So I sang for my hosts, beginning with some of the arias written for the profligate Duke in "Rigoletto." Before long the gypsies began to accompany me, with improvisations, and the whole lot of us sang and danced for a couple of hours. The old woman made me a present of a pair of castanets of antique ivory, and invited me to return to the caves every morning — which I very nearly did, throughout the rest of my stay in Granada. I had to dismiss the policeman because I had no further need of him. Everywhere I went about the city I was attended by a gypsy bodyguard.

Angel Mo' and Her Son, Roland Hayes

My friends from Prague, who had joined me in the
south of Spain, made a leisurely tour of France with
me, on the way back to Paris. We visited Orléans and
venerated relics of the Maid: she had been canonized
only a few years earlier by Benedict XV. We saw a
charming drawing in the museum there, a helmeted head
of a boyish figure, but my friends, for all their piety,
explained that it was probably not a true portrait of
Joan of Arc, as the catalogue claimed. We made a pilgrimage to Lourdes and visited all the châteaux in
Touraine. In a monastery in Avalon we made the Stations of the Cross with the guest master. At the fifth
station, which shows Simon of Cyrene carrying the
Cross, the priest turned to me with a sympathetic smile
and said, "The man who bore our Saviour's Cross was
of your race."

"The skin of our Saviour Himself can hardly be
thought to have been exactly white," I replied.

The priest explained that all men have made Jesus
their own, and Our Lady as well. The Blessed Virgin of
Fra Filippo Lippi is a blonde princess with delicate features and pallid skin. In Barocci's "*Annunziata*," in the
Vatican Library, she is pink and white — and not quite
a lady. In one of the little oratories dedicated to the
Virgin at Avalon, I saw a black Madonna from Africa,
and later in Mexico I saw the black Lord of Chalma. All

(*228*)

I Follow the Black Army

over Mexico a Madonna with a dusky face is venerated by Indians and Spaniards alike. It seems a pity that so many of my race pray that their souls will be white in heaven.

CHAPTER NINE

ℐ Visit ℐtaly and the
U.S.S.R.

IN THE SUMMER of 1925 I met some Italian
people through whom, two years later, I made
my debut in Italy; but before that I spent five
weeks in a dentist's office in Vienna. If gold inlay was
invented in those days, it seems to have been still unknown in Europe. Every day for five weeks I sat for
an hour in an uncomfortable chair, while the dentist
laid gold foil into the painful depths of at least a dozen
of my teeth, and braced myself against the hammering
of a murderous *Klöpfel*. When I arrived at the office
in the morning, the doctor would invert an old-fashioned hourglass. Then he would take up his steel mallet,
peer myopically into my mouth and begin to pound.
I tried to keep my eyes off the hourglass by putting
my mind on the texts and complicated music of the
songs of Charles Tomlinson Griffes, but I always knew
when the end of the hour was at hand. Dr. Gottlieb invariably signalized the last agonizing moments, the

I Visit Italy and the U.S.S.R.

penultimate and ultimate trickle of sand from one pear-shaped bulb to another, by a couple of shattering blows with his hammer, as if to give me a lasting reminder of my engagement to visit his office next morning.

From Vienna I went with Leo Rosenek, whom I was paying daily in marks by the billion, to a quiet hotel on the Pragserwildsee. We settled down (or tried to) to prepare for my third American tour. It was not easy for me to keep at work. My rooms in the otherwise tranquil pension resounded all summer long with echoes from the pounding of the Austrian dentist's mallet. I tried to quiet my nerves by walking about in the fields, talking to the Swiss farmers who tilled them. I was suddenly homesick for the Flatwoods, after all these years.

The headwaiter in the hotel dining room one day pointed out three aristocratic-looking guests from Siena, Signora Giulia Cora and her son-in-law and daughter, the Count and Countess Bourtourline, whose rooms were near the *salon* where I practised. I sent Rosenek to their apartments to present my compliments and inquire whether our rehearsals disturbed them. The Signora replied that on the contrary she and her daughter were in the habit of sitting with their sewing and quietly listening to me. She confirmed her message with a delightful note, and after that we became friends.

Angel Mo' and Her Son, Roland Hayes

When I spoke of my attachment to the country, Count Bourtourline suggested that we take a look at a château which was advertised for sale in Merano, in the near-by Italianized province of Bulzano. We made the steep and dangerous descent one morning and found Merano lying amongst her streams and vineyards in a valley overhung by the Kuechelberg, on whose precipitous slopes stood the ruined castle of Tirolo, the former seat of a noble family which had taken its name from that mountainous region.

The château we wanted to see proved to be no great medieval fortress, but it was of equal antiquity with the Castle Tirolo, and it had seductive appointments. It had been restored in the time of Frederick the Great, whose elegant villa, Sans-Souci, was an inspiration to the then owner, an Austrian gentleman, when he fitted the place up as the bridal residence of an African princess he had taken to wife. We were shown through the house by the proprietor, a German named Ahren, who made a point of repeating its romantic history.

"Your flesh and blood have helped to shape this place," he said. "I think you should now become the lord of the manor."

I asked Herr Ahren to submit his terms in writing, shook hands with him politely, and withdrew with my companions. A contract presently followed me to the Pragserwildsee. I read it and shortly returned it, with

I Visit Italy and the U.S.S.R.

a note to the effect that I had not been able to make up my mind to buy the château, after all. A few days later, Ahren's lawyer drove up to the lake to see me. He informed me that his principal supposed I had already bought the house. I must have had my mind made up, he said, when I shook hands with the owner.

I went hastily to Vienna to see Edward Coumont, my lawyer, who advised me not to sign the contract under any circumstances. It contained a condition purportedly based on ancient Tyrol law, he said, which would permit descendants of the first owner to take the property over whenever they were of a mind to. As for the handshake by which I was said to have committed myself, Coumont said he would send his nephew to Merano to take care of that, and I bought a place close to Paris instead.

I had a lease on a charming house in the department of Seine-et-Oise, the Villa St. Pierre, which was situated in the midst of a seven-acre park at the foot of the Terrace of Henry IV. It had been King Henry's shooting lodge, and after the promulgation of the Edict of Nantes it was incorporated into the royal convert's residence of St. Germain. It was the favorite dwelling place of Gabrielle d'Estrées, who bore Henry so many celebrated children. I decided to buy the villa, at the end of the summer of 1925, and while it was being remodeled and redecorated, I sent to London for furnishings which

Angel Mo' and Her Son, Roland Hayes

I had in storage, bought French antiques with the help of the Duvals and Joseph Salmon — Mme. Duval was Renée Vautiers, the sculptress who made a portrait of me in bronze, from sketches taken while I was singing "Steal Away to Jesus" at the Salle Gaveau — and began to live expansively for the first time in a house of my own.

I had a house in Brookline, but I had never lived in it. On my last trip to America I had bought General Russell's old home on Allerton Street. I had driven past it, for old time's sake, and noticed a "For Sale" sign on the lawn. I telegraphed to Miss Mary Russell, who had moved to California after the death of her parents, to tell her how much it would mean to me to live in a house where I had met with so much kindness and friendship. Miss Mary replied that she could think of no one in the world to whom she would rather sell her father's place. She died not long afterwards, and I think she was happy to know, during her illness, that I was going to live in her house.

I made my third American tour, an enterprise of inordinate length, tedium, and profit, and began the next European season, in the autumn of 1926, with two concerts with the Tivoli Symphony Orchestra of Copenhagen, under the baton of Schnedler-Petersen. I sang Handel, Mozart, Galuppi, Berlioz, Schubert, and Brahms in that sea-locked city, and wrote an article on Negro music for *Politiken*. I was also invited to sing with Mengelberg's orchestra under Monteux in Amsterdam and The Hague, but my managers had booked me for a short and crowded tour of Germany and Austria before my return to America, and I was obliged to go straight to Berlin. I visited Leipzig and Munich once more, and Vienna for the sad, last time.

I liked my Viennese audiences well enough, but I grew tired of the complications which my color invariably caught me up in there. I became weary, after a time, of reading newspaper stories which still began, after five years: *"Ein Neger der Beethoven, Schubert, Brahms, in der Ursprache singt . . ."* even when the critic went on to say *"und . . . fast mochten war sagen . . . auch in der musikalischen Ursprache."* The gossip columnists rarely failed to make a field day of my visits. One of them wrote, during my last one, that the public must not be surprised if, after my departure, they were to see black babies wheeled through the Ring in coroneted prams. I never wanted to go back to Vienna again. Bruno Walter asked me to stay on and sing with the Philharmonic Orchestra there in October, but I had to be in the United States early in that month. I promised, however, to sing with the New York Philharmonic Orchestra under his direction, later on, and that was one of the high spots of my fourth tour of the United States.

I was still too busy, during the American season of 1926–1927, to take conscious and deliberate enjoyment in my work, even though my managers had reduced the number of my concerts from eighty to sixty-five and were collecting on my behalf from two to four thousand dollars for each of them. I always worked hard abroad to be at my best at home, but every year an excess of travel and concertizing broke my spirit and deprived me of spontaneous motion. Sometimes I could recall what had happened only after I took ship for Europe at the end of the season. My secretary would hand me batches of clippings, and I would read that I had been greeted by a "Duke's Mixture" in Charleston, and that Mr. and Mrs. Henry Ford had arrived early and stayed late at my concert in the Masonic Auditorium in Detroit. None of these pieces of intelligence seemed to matter to me very much.

I finally got around to my Italian debut in the autumn of 1927. I went to Siena, where Signora Giulia Cora introduced me to the Conte Chigi Saracini, who kept a school of music in his hereditary palace. The Count gave a soirée at which for the first time I sang a program composed, except for a group of spirituals, entirely of Italian songs.

I Visit Italy and the U.S.S.R.

My interest in Italian music had grown steadily from the days when I first heard recordings of Caruso's voice, and now I could sing all the big and little masters: Caccini, Peri, Monteverdi, Lulli, Galuppi, and the rest. Monteverdi was the originator of the aria in its Italian form — a form which followed naturally upon his experimental elaborations of traditional recitative. Peri was the composer of the first opera, a lost transition piece — it was called "Daphne" — which seems to have developed out of the practice of declamatory singing; and Peri and Caccini together composed "Eurydice," the earliest surviving opera. Monteverdi's "Orfeo" and "Coronation of Poppaea" and Caccini's "Song Book" employ ornamentation quite as exacting as anything composed by their successors. In their own time, in fact, their songs were felt to be so difficult that only eunuchized singers, experienced from childhood in boy choirs, could sing them properly.

Jean Baptiste Lulli, some of whose songs also I sang at Count Chigi's, was born, like Peri, in Florence, and within a year of the older master's death; but he grew up in Paris, where he had been introduced to the court of Louis XIV by the Chevalier de Guise. He composed many of the ballets which a series of official mistresses, particularly Maintenon, regularly arranged for the pleasure of the King, and was rewarded with the royal

(237)

monopoly on the production of French opera. He improved the French style with Italian innovations, such as the enhancement of musical interest in the recitative and the relation of notes to the text — a device of which the French composers had never thought.

I had made a place for two Italians on the program for my first American tour, when I sang Caccini and Galuppi along with Handel and Mozart. Baldassare Galuppi, an eighteenth-century Venetian, is the "Brave Galuppi" of Browning's poem. Browning first invented a toccata for him and then wrote a poem about it. I used the aria *"Evviva Rosa Bella"* from *"Calamità di Curio,"* a song which I have recorded in a recent album, along with the *"Maledetto"* from Monteverdi's *"Scherzi Musicali,"* and a song by Giovanni Maria Bononcini, the father of the more celebrated Giovanni Battista Bononcini who was rival to Handel in London and the master of Scarlatti of Rome.

What with the works of all of these composers, together with a number of others, like the Venetians Lotti and Cesti, I was able to sing, in Siena, straight through the history of Italian music, the sixteenth, seventeenth, and eighteenth centuries, and on into the nineteenth century with Donizetti and Leoncavallo, from whose single successful opera, the brief and tinseled tragedy of the *"Pagliacci,"* I sang the arias of Canio, the unhappy cuckold.

I Visit Italy and the U.S.S.R.

In Florence, by way of contrast, I sang a wholly German program for the exiled Queen Elizabeth of Greece and the local Friends of Music, amongst whom *Lieder* singing was the fashion of the day. Florence in 1927 was one of the first objectives of the annual American tourist invasion. At the Pitti Palace one morning I heard a guide discoursing about the beauty of an old emerald-studded chest. An American gentleman interrupted him to say, "We have had enough history to suit me. Now tell me what that thing would be worth in American dollars." A woman of his party whispered, "Ask him to show us some more statues. I'm very much disappointed in the ones I have seen. They aren't half as pretty as those I saw in a book back home." Thereafter I had greater confidence in my own judgment in artistic matters, however imperfectly disciplined my taste had been.

My Italian friends professed to be interested in my prospective tour of Russia. Count Chigi counseled me to take plenty of furs, coats and capes, and fur-lined boots, and to beware of the Communists. I was reminded of an interview I had given in Boston, of which the published version said that I had fortunately not yet taken to wearing fur coat and spats, but I made notes of certain requirements and later gave orders to furriers in Paris for the equipment which Count Chigi thought I should have.

(*239*)

Angel Mo' and Her Son, Roland Hayes

It was at Count Chigi's dinner party that William Lawrence, who had been traveling with me for several years, told me he had decided not to go with me to Russia. The end was in sight of a long and fruitful collaboration. I cabled to Percival Parham, who joined me shortly in Paris and accompanied me at home and abroad until his death in 1938. He was a wonderful friend.

I gave the last of my concerts with Lawrence in London in November and December of that year. It had been two or three years since I had sung in England and I was delighted to find that I had not been quite forgotten there. Wigmore Hall was filled three or four times, for a series of recitals in which I sang through a considerable part of my repertoire. The fact that I had relaxed enough to pleasure myself a little seemed to have improved the quality of my singing. My conscience, which had been well cultivated by my mother, had bothered me, I must confess, in Spain and Italy, where I had spent more time in society and away from my work than ever before in my life, and it was with not a little relief that I read in *The Times* that my voice was thought to have a new vocal color. I had taken the devil's counsel, but I finally had this advantage over Launcelot Gobbo, that I was able to satisfy a kind of hard conscience as well.

I Visit Italy and the U.S.S.R.

I suppose it is true, as one of the London critics had said three or four years earlier, that my interpretation of the brighter songs always seemed to be tinged with melancholy. The truth is that I was happy during my years on the Continent and I could now approach cheerful music more cheerfully. The Parisian journal *Comoedia* once published Renée Vautiers's sculpture of me over the caption: "*C'est Paris qui l'attire et c'est à Paris qu'il revient toujours*"; and that expressed my sentiments exactly. I do not mean that in my earliest years I had been sorry for myself. I simply mean that walking softly in white society used to be, by and large, a somewhat melancholy adventure.

Show me a man — a singer, a painter, a poet — who is indifferent to compliments, and I will prove to you that he has a heart of cork. People who address themselves to the public live on the praise of the public as well as on its purse. And I suppose that everybody in the public eye looks for some particular form of recognition. For myself, a direct statement of the single appraisal that I wanted in those days was more to be treasured than learned essays about my techniques and programs, because, I fancy, it corresponded with the resolution I had taken, back in Chattanooga, after I had heard Caruso. It was worth going back to London to read these simple words once more: "He is a great artist."

(*241*)

II

On my way from England to Russia I sang in Amsterdam, where the people liked best the florid French music and the Negro spirituals. I went through a kind of revival of religious enthusiasm there, in that Protestant country, and perhaps I sang the spirituals with new feeling. I had not been neglecting the music of my race, I was singing it faithfully everywhere, but in Catholic Europe I had doubtless given the effect of setting European music artistically above it. Now the music of my own people filled my heart and mind again. I had early appreciated the religious quality of the songs my ancestors sang, and had long since, with the help of Dr. Lierhammer's intuition, come to feel that the slave composers were moved by the same fiery Spirit that inspired Bach and Schubert. But now that I was maturing as an artist, I began with greater conviction to present the spirituals as works of art. It is their rare combination of art and spirituality that makes great music out of songs which appear on the surface to be so artless.

The Negro slaves had been put to the same school of humility that produced the Catholic saints. When they became Christians, they approached their God humbly. Even in their music they did not dare to speak to Him directly. They spoke to Him in quiet, trailing melodies, adorned with hundreds of delicate little turns and semi-quavers. Their use of quarter and eighth notes was a part of their instinctive modesty in the presence of the divine Spirit they venerated. Their eyes closed, their black faces turned from the consuming Presence, they poured out their helpless love and guileless confidence with trembling voice — as though they were hoping against hope that the God Whom they dared not approach directly could thus be won through indirection. In such a way they asked for deliverance from their sufferings and peace at the last.

In Amsterdam I sang "Were You There?" without accompaniment. While my great-grandfather's version of the death of Christ had been a kind of divine tragedy, full of implications of pain and sorrow, the spiritual "Were You There?" sublimates and glorifies the Way of the Cross. Jesus does not so much die as conquer death.

> Were you there when they crucified my Lord?
> Oh, sometimes it causes me to tremble, tremble —
> Were you there when they crucified my Lord?

I felt that night in Amsterdam that the Crucifixion was taking place in my heart once more, and I was glad when a man told me that Christ's Sacrifice had been renewed in him. I caught a new glimpse of my mother's figure of the Christian priesthood. So it is, I felt, that through music sin dies, and the Word becomes flesh and dwells among us.

At this high peak of religious inspiration I set out for the Union of Socialist Soviet Republics, where, I had been told, religion itself had been crucified. We were to be official guests of the Soviet Union, Parham and Jordan and I, charged with helping to celebrate the tenth anniversary of the creation of the Red Army — but we had to wait a month in Berlin for our visas. At last, on January 28, 1928, the calendarian, although not the official, anniversary of the first Red Army exploit, we received the necessary passports and papers, boarded the evening train for Moscow, and spent the first night of our journey in a succession of customs examinations. We rode all the next day through the flat, white fields of Poland and arrived at the Russian frontier after dark. Polish inspectors had relieved me of every scrap of writing in my luggage, so that nothing of interest could possibly have been left to the Russians, who nevertheless continued to inspect my possessions for the space of two hours.

We liked the Russian railway coaches which awaited us at the border. They were large and warm and comfortable — although poor Parham was distressed to discover that they were not exactly private. He found that

I Visit Italy and the U.S.S.R.

he was expected to share a sleeping compartment with a strange woman. From the dining car the next morning, we looked out upon the snowy Russian landscape. It was studded with clumps of miniature firs and birches, with here and there a village of low huts which looked as though they had been plowed into the ground against the ravages of wind. I remember being baffled by the signs I saw in railway stations, but I consoled myself by reflecting that if I could not speak the language of the country, I should not be in danger of saying something I might regret.

We arrived in Moscow on the afternoon of the third day out of Berlin and were taken at once to the Grand Hotel, an enormous and expensive caravanserai where foreigners were evidently expected to spend as much as they could earn in the country. I put on my fur boots and greatcoat and went for a drive in a droshky.

I was booked in advance for ten concerts in Russia, of which the first was scheduled for the day after my arrival. When I started early in the evening to retire, in order to get thoroughly rested for it, I felt a bad cold coming on. My dearly bought bed, when I tried to take refuge in it, was as unyielding and inhospitable as a kitchen table. It was not only hard, it was nearly bare of clothing as well. I was numb with cold and began to

(*245*)

sniffle. Much too uncomfortable to sleep, I lay in bed and read Emerson's essay on "Self-Reliance."

My copy of the *Essays* was as well-thumbed as my mother's Bible. I had found homely truths in it to strengthen and comfort me, and many words of wise counsel for a lonely and difficult life. "There is a time in every man's education when he arrives at the conviction that envy is ignorance; that imitation is suicide; that he must take himself for better, for worse, as his portion. . . ." Again, "the only right is what is after my constitution, the only wrong what is against it." These rhythmical clauses sounded to me like Revelation.

My mother had chosen the hard way of duty for herself and tried to send her children out into the world with a sense of mission. I often looked into Emerson for reminders of my duty. "What I must do is all that concerns me, not what the people think. . . . But do your work and I shall know you, do your work and you shall reinforce yourself."

Emerson is a stern master for our day — although it would do none of us harm to begin reading him again — but my ways were early patterned after those of a still earlier epoch, and I took readily to his teaching. Alone and ill in Russia, so many days and miles from home, I reread his variation on a theme from Milton: "The soul is no traveler; a wise man stays at home, and when his necessities, his duties on any occasion, call him from his house, or into foreign lands, he is at home still, and shall make men sensible by the expression of his countenance that he goes the missionary of wisdom and virtue, and visits cities and men like a sovereign and not like an interloper or a valet."

I spent the next day in my chilly bed, and in the late afternoon, when I got up to dress for my concert, the temperature of my room was well below freezing. I was shaking with fever and fainting with weariness when I walked out upon the platform of the Moscow Conservatory, and I had to sing over a bad head cold. I had to will myself out of my weakness, and fall back on tried techniques to take care of the cold.

Sir George Henschel had taught me a lesson, back in 1921, about singing over a cold. I had told him one day that I could not take my lesson because my head was stopped up.

"That is no reason for not singing," he said. "You don't sing *with* a cold, you sing around it."

Although I believe a singer's mental attitude towards indisposition is of first importance – he must never allow himself to be dismayed by it – I have developed a set of exercises calculated to improve the circulation of my blood throughout the areas affected by catarrh. I relax my neck and tilt my head downwards toward my chest, then over my left shoulder, and then to the right. I make these motions for five minutes at a time, before a concert and during the intermissions. And sometimes I sip egg white, stiffly beaten with a little sugar and the juice of half a lemon. With my head and throat thus momentarily cleared, I try to forget my aches and pains in my music.

I was greeted by the Muscovites with half-hearted applause, on the occasion of which I am speaking. They looked bewildered and deceived, as though they had expected to see a black giant with bulging muscles and ape-like features; or perhaps, I thought, they had expected a trumpet and saw only a pitch-pipe. They heard my first group out in silence, colder than the silence of Leipzig.

The second group, the German songs, broke the audience down a little. I sang encore after encore, and then everybody went out to drink tea. My spirits rose, but somewhat timidly, for I still felt ill and weak and cold. It was Emerson who persuaded me to return and sing the Russian group which I had laboriously prepared over a number of months — songs of Tchaikovsky, Slonimsky, Taneieff, and Gretchaninoff.

I took fifteen bows after the Russian music, each one draining my small remaining store of strength. I did not dare to give an encore lest I should be unable to finish the program with the spirituals, and after the concert, when I was greeted by people from all over the world, I was too tired to speak. I had to refuse an invitation to take tea with a plump little bearded man who turned out to be the rising statesman Litvinoff. The concert manager's startled reproof to my manners lent intelligibility to the faint look of incredulity I thought I had detected on the little man's face when I excused myself.

While I was quietly taking my supper in my hotel sitting room, after the concert, a waiter handed me a card engraved with an interesting name and address. I received the visitor, a young East Indian poet named Herin-dranath, who spoke to me of India and the Mahatma Gandhi. A month later I received a letter signed by Gandhi himself: —

DEAR FRIEND [he wrote],

Mr. H. Chattopadyaya writes to me saying that you are likely to visit India in the near future. If you do and if you visit Gujarit please regard this little Ashram as your home.

I began at once to prepare for a visit to India, to Gandhi's "little Ashram," but the Mahatma was soon thrown into prison and I did not go.

My new friend Herin came back to the hotel the

morning after my Moscow debut and translated some
oddly phrased notices from the socialist newspapers.
According to the critic Braudo, I had introduced my
audience to an "active co-experience" in the tragedy of
an exploited race; I had proved, he said, that the American Negroes were ready to take their part in the inter-
national struggle for freedom. I was not a little surprised
by this political interpretation of my singing, until I
discovered that in the Russian translations printed in
my programs the spirituals had been put through a
secular revision which made propaganda out of the
original evangelical texts.

I came upon this singular fact during an intermission
in the second of my concerts in Leningrad, when a
young woman visited me in the Green Room and asked
me to show her the English texts of the Negro songs
I had sung at my first recital. I asked her if she would
mind getting permission to look at them from the commissar who went about with me everywhere. With that
gentleman's consent, I handed her a sheaf of the printed
texts, which she began at once to read aloud.

"I knew it! I knew it!" she exclaimed excitedly, when
she had run through a few verses.

She was so nearly hysterical that I became very
nervous.

"What did you know?" I asked.

I Visit Italy and the U.S.S.R.

"I knew you were singing about God," she said, and her eyes were shining.

"But didn't you already know that?" I asked. "Translations of the texts are printed in the program."

"Has anyone told you what those translations say?" she inquired, and proceeded to give me a literal rendering of the "translation" of "Go Down, Moses."

The twenty-five original verses of that spiritual recite the history of the people of Israel, beginning with their redemption from "ole Pharaoh," down in "Egypt lan'," and continuing with a paraphrase of the Biblical account of their wanderings, up to the fall of Jericho. According to the Soviet version, I had been singing a history of the Negro's effort to liberate himself from slavery. And "Deep River," a song of religious aspiration if ever there was one, had become, in proletarian hands, a dreary narrative about Negroes picnicking on the banks of the Jordan River.

Back in Moscow, Herin took me to visit the Church of Our Saviour, a Moorish edifice and one of a small number of churches open — and then only on Sunday — for the celebration of religious services. We went in on a weekday, paid our entrance fees as though we were visiting a museum, and spent an hour feeling our way back through the generations of the spiritual life of the community which had built and maintained it. I thought

(*251*)

again of Emerson, who liked "the silent church before the service begins, better than any preacher." I saw no hymn books, no doctrinal texts. I determined then and there that on the next occasion of singing the spirituals in Moscow, I should endeavor so to make God shine through them, with the faith of my mother and her kind, that the banal and coldly humanistic texts, printed by some atheistic commissar, should not entirely obscure their spiritual meaning. And so, with God's help, I was able to do. After my next concert a ruling member of the Communist Party admitted to me that she had experienced a "peculiar feeling" which, as a professing atheist, she was unable to describe.

"I am sure, however," she quickly added, "that my feelings do not correspond to any spiritual reality, and I do not expect them to last very long."

A young Chicago Negro named Jones, a student at the University of Moscow, tried to convert Herin and me to the new political philosophy, but everywhere I looked the effects of Communist doctrine seemed to me so bleak and so unlovely that I was not a good subject for persuasion.

I was taken to see a government-sponsored play entitled "The Window Facing the Village." There was practically no sense of theater in that production. There was no curtain, for example. The argument of the piece was projected upon a moving-picture screen, the actors moved silently into their places on the stage, the lights went up and the performance began. There was no play of the imagination, no tug of fancy: it was all as matter-of-fact as a cold-storage warehouse. The author of the play intended to show that the Party had established schools in rural districts everywhere and had carried scientific methods from the factories to the farms. What he wrote was simply an account of a forum in which a forensic address was broken up into parts and assigned to players representative of various proletarian types.

Opera in Moscow was hardly more artistic than the theater, although the opera house itself retained something of its Czarist magnificence, with its frescoes and draperies and richly upholstered seats. It was packed with working people on the night we attended a performance of "Boris Godunoff" — men and women who had come straight from mill and factory, still dressed in their dirty blue and black blouses and aprons.

I like Moussorgsky's opera immensely, and I appreciated what I could remember on that occasion of the literate text of Pushkin's poetical tale — my Russian acquaintances repeatedly reminded me that the poet's great-grandfather was an Abyssinian — but the singing was only perfunctory. Still, I was contented to sit through the prologue and the four long acts for the sake of the music, and I remained quietly in my seat until Boris died in the arms of his son.

When I rose up to leave, somebody tugged at my sleeve. The performance was not over. The orchestra played a *divertissement* which I could not recognize as having come from the pen of Moussorgsky, and there filed onto the stage a troupe of actors got up as soldiers and beggars. They squatted around an electric campfire while one of their number angrily sang an impromptu recitative. The evening did not come to an end until all their voices had been joined in some defamatory chorus which the audience enthusiastically cheered.

As it happened, the only artistic event I ever did attend in a Russian theater was Stanislavsky's production of (of all things!) Maeterlinck's "Bluebird." Largely through the use of effective lighting, that dated whimsy was brought to life; but what the factory hands thought of it I could not guess.

I gave my second Moscow concert on the evening of February 7. I was feeling fit and in good voice. I sang the *Lieder* and the spirituals according to the program, and then I gave my audience what they really wanted to hear — aria after aria, until late into the night. I was satisfied at last with my reception in Moscow and ready to tour the southern provinces. The following evening we started out, Herin, Parham, Jordan, and my Russian

manager and I, on the twenty-four-hour journey to
Kiev.

III

The halls and chambers of our hotel in Kiev were
hung with remnants of Czarist luxury. There were ele-
gantly fitted bathrooms through whose pipes no water
ran. There was an impressive staff of servants who took
no orders from the guests. There were elaborate menus
in the dining room, but in the kitchen there was no
congruity of food. A boiled egg, a plate of bread and
butter, and a pot of tea would appear at intervals, the tea
two hours after the egg, the bread gray and bitter.

The automobile which came to take me to the concert hall was a shabby vehicle which had been produced
in the Noachic epoch of the history of Detroit. We
insinuated ourselves into its narrow seats. It did not
budge. Presently it coughed, but its movement was only
lateral and vertical. Herin and I held onto the back
of the front seat, hoping to keep body and soul of the
car together, while the chauffeur called for help. A
throng of men and boys crouched on the running boards
and pushed us at last through the snowy streets to the
hall.

It was not inspiring to sing to an audience of snigger-
ing peasants who behaved as though they had come to

inspect an African savage. I felt that they were resent-
ful because I neither looked nor sang like an inhabitant
of the jungle. The people out front were the savages,
actually, and I had to tame them. It took precisely two
exhausting hours to do it, but when I had indeed made
friends with them, I was scarcely permitted to leave.
Crowds followed the antediluvian coach all the way to
my hotel and demanded an impromptu concert in the
courtyard in the morning.

At the railway station, the next day, we elbowed our
way through a throng of beggars and boarded a sleeping
car for Kharkov. We found ourselves in what appeared
to be a well-appointed compartment; but we had learned
to be suspicious of mechanical contrivances in the interior of Russia. We fiddled with the switch buttons,
but nothing happened. The porter lighted a candle,
after dark, and set it in a small glass cage where it
flickered dimly. We turned the spigot over the wash-
basin, this way and that, and not a drop came out. We
asked for drinking water, of which there was none
aboard, not even bottled water which we might have
bought. Our dinner was served chronologically throughout the night, carrots and potatoes at ten o'clock, a fillet
of beef a half hour later, a pot of tea at midnight. In
the morning we washed in mineral water we had pur-
chased ourselves at a wayside station, and dried our

hands and faces with our handkerchiefs. We brewed our tea with sparkling water.

Herin and I spent the afternoon walking the streets of Kharkov, attended by a large section of the population. The city was a fascinating architectural hybrid, a mélange of Gothic, Moorish, Teutonic, and Byzantine, with here and there a Soviet design to preach the Communist gospel of utility and hard economy.

When I stood before my audience in the evening, in a decaying concert hall, I was made to feel like a collection of prehistoric bones on exhibition in a glass case. I had been brought to the people by their government — issued, so to speak, like food and clothing; and their faces seemed to me to wear an appearance of stupidity and weariness, such as I had observed when I saw them in the daytime, immobilized in queues upon the street. There was something pathetic in their astonishment when they discovered that they were getting more out of my concert than their ration cards had led them to expect. I felt that I was giving them relief, for a little while, from the sordidness of their living arrangements: the close-packed sleeping; the endless cooking of two or three families sharing a single stove in a steam-filled room; the victualing with undernourishing commodities because everything of value had to be exported in the interest of exchange.

Angel Mo' and Her Son, Roland Hayes

After the concert I went with my companions to a restaurant which advertised a balalaika orchestra. To honor our entrance, the leader swung his band into American jazz. We took a glass of hot tea and a very small supper. In fact, I was hungry all the time I was in Russia.

The Moscow manager was inclined to treat me like a music box which he could wind up and set down to sing anywhere, at any time. Wherever we had a successful concert, he promptly booked a return engagement. I was so overcome by the misery and desolation of the country, and by my own acute discomfort, that I was anxious only to fill my scheduled engagements and withdraw. Except for two events which occurred in Kharkov, I think I should not have had the heart to go on to distant Rostov.

Out of a crowd of people standing around the door of the Hotel Rouge, when we left to go to the railway station, there emerged an old man with a beaming, wrinkled face and eyes like diamonds. He plucked my cloak and said, "Are you going away, Mister? Very good, Mister, thank you, Mister."

I asked him if he had heard my concert.

"*Ja, es war wunderschön,*" he said. He had heard it by radio, through an unauthorized broadcast. "You come again? Maybe next week?"

I Visit Italy and the U.S.S.R.

"Not next week, my friend," I replied. "Perhaps next year."

A cloud passed over the old man's face, his eyes filled with tears.

"Good-bye, Mister, thank you, Mister," he said, and hobbled away.

The other bright spot in my visit to Kharkov was a ride in a *troika* drawn by three fine dappled grays abreast. The *izshveshik*, who wore a padded coat with enormous sleeves which served his passengers for windshield, tucked us into the sled under a great weight of black bearskin robes and drove us dramatically up and down the city. I had never in my life enjoyed such exhilarating transportation. I wished that we could go all the way to Rostov in that comfortable splendor. Indeed, I should have been glad to cancel the Rostov concert altogether, in order to ride around in Kharkov all day long, nestled in thick furs, breathing the crisp, fresh air, and enchanted by the wintry sparkle of the flashing avenues.

We had the sense to equip ourselves with a basket of bread and butter and sliced ham and preserves for the journey to Rostov. Howard Jordan bought a drinking cup. I carried a supply of wax candles in my handbag, and Parham filched a teaspoon from the Hotel Rouge. The train to Rostov carried a sleeping car only three times a week, and since my concert fell upon one of the intervening days we had to sleep sitting up.

Whenever the train came to a stop at a station, beggars swarmed into the carriages before the passengers could descend. Many of the mendicants looked like men and women of race and education, but poverty had made thieves and robbers of them all. Parham had his shoes snatched out of his hands while he sat bent over in his compartment, ready to put them on.

Most of the sidewalks and pavements of Rostov had disappeared under a flood, and as much of the city as had not been possessed by the deluge was overrun by convivial commissars. We found sorry quarters in an inn provisioned with neither heat nor food. We were grateful when the northbound train pulled into the station the next day, equipped with *wagon lits* bound straight for Moscow.

When I read today of the beleaguered cities along the Eastern Front, south to the Sea of Azov and north to Leningrad, in my mind I see them as they used to be. I am filled with respectful wonder when I hear how the Russian people, whose inexperience had produced nothing but disorder then, whose farms and cities were incapable of supplying goods for ordinary daily needs, have been able in this war to muster such abundantly

implemented and bravely organized resistance to ordered German might.

On our way back to the capital of the Soviet Union,
Herin tried to cheer me up by teaching me the "Welcome Song" of India. He wrote out a phonetic trans-
literation, which went something like this: —

> *Shevaia nava home,*
> *Shevaia nama ha,*
> *Shevaia nava home,*
> *Nama shevaia home.*

He wanted me to be able to sing it to the Mahatma, he
said, on the visit to India he was determined I should
make. I predetermined the success of my last appearance in Moscow by preparing a program with plenty
of flamboyant music. I sang most of the arias from the
five operas I had not quite forgotten, and on the cover
of my program I printed a picture for which I had
posed on the shores of Lake Lucerne, in a cotton shirt
unbuttoned at the neck. I looked for all the world like
a fellow traveler.

Many letters followed me out of Russia. A kind of
round robin was composed, section by section, by a
group of university professors, one of whom wrote that
he sat for many hours over his dictionary to produce
the page and a half of his contribution. It is a touching

letter, full of Platonic reference to Goodness, Truth, and Beauty. Another epistle, written during Holy Week, pathetically concludes, "What a great event Easter used to be amongst us!"

A melancholy, impractical, and childlike race, the Russians — or so they seemed to me then — and yet how, in so many ways, like my own people. But today I see that they have grown strong, they have become giants overnight, in the preservation of their freedom. How long shall we Negroes, on our side, continue to grow weaker in imitative bondage? How long, oh Lord, how long?

CHAPTER TEN

I Renew My Vow at Angel Mo' Farm

Done made my vow to the Lord,
I never will turn back.
I will go, I shall go,
To see what the end will be.

IT WAS no Negro chiliast who taught me, in 1929, that the end of an age was coming. That bad news was revealed to me by a Wall Street prophet, one of a company of New York bankers I met on board ship on my way to Paris after the most remunerative tour I ever made. Those gentlemen were much more interested in my earnings than in my art. They scolded me for knowing so little about my investments, which I had to confess I had left in the hands of indifferent agents. One of them took pains to advise me to hurry back to Boston on the next boat, so that I might put my affairs in shape before the impending crash. I took his advice. I did indeed go back — although not for long; but even so, I was too late to do myself much good. I exchanged a few characteristically Bostonian securities, like hotel holding-company certificates and imaginary shares in a Swedish match king's properties, for small parcels of overpriced real estate; but still the October crash, when it overtook me, caught me badly. I found it difficult then not to "turn back" upon my career, because so many of my hopes were dissipated.

In spite of the horrid drain of expense, of which a good deal was incurred by a polite form of bribery that enabled me to travel with some degree of decency, I had put by a considerable fortune which I had thought to use for the training of young Negro artists. We Negroes, I had said to myself, have been parasitic long enough. Born and reared in a state of dependence, we have been pauperized by being too long on the receiving end of financial and cultural transactions. I proposed to use Negro money, for a change, to build Negro reputations.

I wanted to invite promising Negro boys and girls, painters and poets and musicians, to my farm in Georgia, where, always close to the soil, they could be tested for vocation: exposed to the arts in native and imported forms, and trained in the direction of their several propensities. I thought of making my house in Boston a kind of hostel to which boys and girls from the South could go for their intermediate education. After that, my villa in France was to have been open to the cream of the crop — those young people whose early promise had begun to be realized in Boston. In my mind I was repeating, of course, the pattern of my own life, but the program appealed to me as being economical of time. After 1929, it seemed unlikely that I should ever be able to carry out this scheme. Still, I was unwilling to allow myself to be broken by disaster. After all, I owned my farm and my houses and I vowed I would make no permanent retreat.

Although I did not give up my house in Paris until 1932, it was a great comfort to me to know that at home I had a farm to which I could momentarily return. I had begun life there, and it was not impossible to believe that other people could still go out into the world from the same place. In the meanwhile, I could go there myself, when life became too difficult, and put my hand to the plow: —

> Mary had a golden chain,
> Every link was Jesus' name.
> Keep yo' hand on the plow,
> Hold on! Hold on!

I have no doubt that the thought of home lent some new nostalgic quality to my singing of the Negro music, for it was just before I came back to America to live that Joseph Baruzi, one of the Paris critics, wrote that I "mounted the spirituals as though they were horses and galloped on them to Paradise."

Angel Mo' and Her Son, Roland Hayes

The idea of buying the farm where my mother was born had occurred to me in 1926. A year or two earlier I had crossed the Atlantic from Europe with Ignace Paderewski, on the *S.S. Paris,* and I appeared with him in a concert for the Seamen's Fund. Mr. Myron T. Herrick, our Ambassador to France, was master of ceremonies, and in his introduction he made me sound like a more important figure in the world of music than I had really yet become. What the King and Queen of England had not been able to do for me in America, in the space of five years, the frequently decorated author of *Rural Credits* accomplished overnight. His commendation, transmitted by a gentleman aboard who hailed from Atlanta, got me an invitation to sing at last in the capital of my native state. In November, 1926, I was received by a mixed audience of seven thousand people in the Atlanta Auditorium.

The day after that long deferred debut I motored up to Calhoun, the county seat of Gordon County, picked up a boyhood friend, Allen Henson, the district attorney, and drove over to Little Row, which by that time the postal authorities called Curryville. Not a stick or splinter remained of our old cabin in the Flatwoods. Three cedar trees had survived from the grove which used to screen our house from the lane leading to Mount Zion Church, and a grapevine smothered a pecan tree which was all that remained of a tidy little orchard of nuts and fruit. But with the eyes of my mind I rebuilt the old barnyard and my heart repeopled it.

There, three paces from the stump of the hickory tree where Pa used to weave riven white-oak splints into baskets for cotton pickers, I stand shivering in the thinning darkness. I hold a lantern to guide Ma's sufficient fingers to the teats of our rawboned cow. Because it is winter, I have my last year's brogans on, but they are shorn now of their brass tips, and my cold, bare toes poke through them, suffering an exposure the more cruel because it is dictated by poverty and not by fashion. I long to go in to the warm hearth where — surely this is a holiday from school! — we shall presently be carding and spinning and batting the cotton we picked in September, while Pa talks Indian language and roasts sweet potatoes in the hot ashes.

I hear Ma say, "You cain't go in, son, until you shuck some of that corn and take it up to Rocky Creek."

Squire Kemp's old rock gristmill is up on Rocky Creek, two or three miles away, but it seems a thousand. I shuck the corn and get up astride old Molly, I ride to the mill and wait my turn, perishing with hunger. I watch Squire Kemp's men feed the corn between two stone wheels which grind and grind unendingly, while water tumbles over the dam in a noisy cataract from a lake in the valley back of the mill. I think I am going to be there most all day, and I wonder if it will be dark before I get home; for then I shall likely see headless men riding their horses in the graveyard, and rabbits cutting the buck and wing on a tombstone.

If I get home before dark I shall go fishing with Robert in a small stream which the mill rush makes when it flows past the bottom land below our farm. We shall dig for dirt worms back of the compost bin and catch some nice perch for supper. I am glad it is not Sunday. Things happen to boys who go fishing on Sunday. I remember the time I disobeyed my mother and went down to the brook with my Cousin Solomon Mann on a Sabbath afternoon. We hooked a big fish which leaped up out of the water and glared at us with eyes as red as fire.

"Th'ow it away, th'ow it away, Roland!" Solomon cried. "That fish is the Devil, come to get us for fishing on Sunday!"

We flung the red-eyed fish back into the creek and ran to the cabin for dear life. When Ma came home from church we were under the grapevine, quaking because of our sins.

Now the season changes. We plant and hoe and harvest. Ma gives us beans and onions and tomatoes for dinner. She sends us out to pick ripe Concord grapes which she will make into jelly, and if we come in with our lips and tongues stained with grape juice, she cures us of dawdling by means of a few strokes of her thin hickory switch.

The whipping was so realistic that it wakened me from my dream of old times. I rubbed my eyes and turned to my companion.

"Do any of the Manns still live hereabouts, Mr. District Attorney?" I asked.

"Old Joe Mann who owned your mother lives up yonder in Sugar Valley, no more'n five-six miles from here," he replied.

Mr. Henson and I drove over to the valley and found Joe Mann's dejected two-room shanty. It was perched precariously on a red-clay bank, overlooking a nearly impassable lane. A shabby old man came to the door. He took us in to see his pitiful sick wife, and then we went out into the yard to talk and have our picture taken.

"I have come to tell you," I said, "that I'm going to buy up the place your family had in Curryville, and I shall fit up a house where you and your wife may spend the rest of your days together."

I did buy the Mann plantation, with Lawyer Henson's help, as I had determined to do directly I came out of my barnyard musings, and I named it in memory of my mother: Angel Mo' Farm. But Mr. and Mrs. Mann were laid away in the grave before I could fit up the house which I had not thought of until I saw how they had come down in the world.

II

The depression did not immediately upset the plans my managers had for me, as I had at first supposed it would. They booked me, in fact, for two or three more crowded seasons. Returning annually from my home in Paris, I covered the country, North, South, East, and West: and particularly the South, so that I could keep my eye on Angel Mo' Farm; and the North, so that I could keep track of my Cousin Alzada. When I went to New York in 1931, I found Alzada ill and lonely in a hospital ward to which she had been removed from her unquiet room in Harlem. I carried her off to Brookline and left her in my house, under a housekeeper's care, while I went on my customary tour of the West. I came back to find the house transformed. It was a home now, for the first time — winsome enough in appearance, and comfortable enough in its use, to reconcile me to the probable abandonment of my villa in Paris; and ordered with such tact and economy that I could not bear to think of the impermanence of the arrangements. Above all, Alzada herself was well again, and happy and lovable.

I begged her to marry me and promised her that if she would put up with the necessity of my traveling, I would lay everything I had at her feet — knowing full well how much more she, who had already begun so engagingly to identify herself with my life, had to give me. I thought of the last part of *Faust*, which I had lately read in Vienna: "The eternal woman lifts us up." I had leaned heavily upon women in my time. Now, uniquely since my mother's death, I was to find myself raised up by woman's undistracted love.

I had to go back to California, within a few days of my proposal, to sing in the Hollywood Bowl. We went down to Angel Mo' and persuaded my brother Robert to drive us out to the Coast. When we reached Southern California, Alzada and I slipped away and were secretly married. That was in September, 1932.

A year or two earlier, after a concert in Georgia, Robert, who had driven over from the farm in my new Chevrolet, appeared in the Green Room in a polished boiled shirt and presented me to a handsome young woman and a preacher of his acquaintance.

"We want to see what it's like to stand out there on the stage," he said.

I took them out behind the footlights.

(*271*)

Angel Mo' and Her Son, Roland Hayes

"This looks O.K.," said Robert. "Let's get going."

The preacher took a little book out of his pocket and performed a marriage on the spot. That is why Alzada and I got married without telling Robert, but I was so delighted to have done something without any publicity that we kept our marriage secret for quite a long time.

Our daughter, Africa Franzada, who was born two years later, is a quaint little sprite of a girl, so refined and delicate that if rough hands were to touch her she might easily be shattered. She is full of the intuitions and perceptions of her grandfather and inherits a good share of my mother's mysticism and practical sense. She lives in a world of her own creation, in which she is entirely self-directed and where knowledge comes to her apparently without process. Roger Quilter used to say to me, "Roland, there is no logic in your thinking. How is it that there is logic in what you do?" Africa finds the answers to her problems with the same immediacy, but we often have to let her lead us into her own world before we can see how right the answers invariably are.

There is more humor in Africa's world than there was in mine, and I am grateful for that grace. When she assumes a character to play, sometimes for days at a time, the character of a princess or a prima donna, she is exacting equally of herself and her audience, but always there are overtones of impish gaiety. Like my father, she has a great gift for mimicry. She spares neither kith nor kin the sharp, amusing caricature of gesture, inflection, and phrase. She loves especially to tease her daddy. On a Sunday morning not long ago, while I was touching up my wife's pantry shelves with a paint brush, she came and stood in the pantry door, grinned at me bewitchingly, and sang a ditty which I had learned years ago in Sunday School: —

> Ain't it a shame to work on Sunday, ain't it a shame,
> When you got Monday, Tuesday, Wednesday,
> When you got Thursday, Friday, Saturday,
> Ain't it a shame to work on Sunday, ain't it a shame?

Africa has a finely imaginative musical talent. By the time she was three years old, she had absorbed most of the Schumann *Dichterliebe*, which I sang frequently in those years. One day while I was rehearsing them with Percival Parham, she slid down the banister from the upstairs hall and into the music room. She turned a couple of cartwheels and said, "But Daddy! That piece you are singing goes like this!"

She hummed a phrase in the little voice she was possessed of, and so it did go like that. I was wrong and she was right, and her ear remains nearly infallible.

A month or two after Africa's fourth birthday, I introduced a young singer, a soprano, to a company of friends in my studio, and she sang, amongst other things, the Mozart "Alleluia." Two weeks later, after dinner with my daughter's Godmother, Africa announced a concert. She closed a pair of portieres which hung between entrance hall and parlor, made a formal entrance, and acknowledged our applause with a new little bow in which I vaguely recognized a hint of the young woman who had sung in my house. She then launched out into the "Alleluia" aria, pouring out the cascaded phrases one after another in accurate pitch and sequence, if with some natural inadequacy of tone.

"But darling, you don't know that piece," my wife protested, when Africa had taken her bow.

"Don't you remember when that lady sang it?" Africa reminded her mother. And the tone of her voice suggested that nobody but an idiot could forget a piece of music he had heard.

We do not yet know if our child will make a career of music, and if she does, whether she will sing or play. At the moment, she likes to compose at the piano, while I write down the notes. It saddens my wife and me that we cannot give her the advantages she requires without exposing her to unhappiness. We hope for her sake that she will choose the more private life of the composer, but if she wants to be a concert artist we shall not stand in her way. She will then have to make her own vow to the Lord and not turn back.

I Renew My Vow at Angel Mo' Farm

If the seasons of 1930 and 1931, the sixth and seventh seasons of transcontinental touring, closed another of the separable chapters of my life, the year 1932 began a new one full of deep personal satisfaction. For nearly ten years I had sung to rich and famous people, and had known something of wealth and fame myself; but most of that time I had lived a kind of melancholy eremite. In the more natural disposition of marriage and fatherhood, I found emotional fulfillment. And on the farm I was able to renew my attachment to the soil which gave me birth. Instead of faring from a luxurious and not quite personal French villa, to make anxious and expensive tours, I was able to go out buoyed up from Angel Mo', appear here and there without pretension, and return to wholesome family life. I resolved to sing only as the spirit moved me, and especially to people who wanted spiritual refreshment. I began to give recital-conferences in colleges and universities throughout the land, appealing to students, whose ears are dinned by thousands of juke boxes, not to let themselves grow deaf to the serious music of the past.

III

In 1935, to my surprise, I reached a new peak of experience in singing to large audiences at low prices, particularly in the coastal cities of the West. Poor and unfashionable people of all races came to hear me, and many of them stopped to say that they had liked the first concert they had ever heard. In the midst of that season I was invited to sing at the dedication of the Theodore Roosevelt Memorial, to represent the Negro race. I remembered the furore which followed when President Roosevelt had Booker T. Washington to lunch at the White House. I also remembered that during my student days in Boston he complimented me when I sang "Deep River" and "Go Down, Moses" on some official occasion. I offered those spirituals for the dedication, but one of the Roosevelts asked for his father's favorite song, "The Battle Hymn of the Republic."

The imposing memorial, with a pink granite face modeled on the imperial architecture of Rome, was opened by President Franklin D. Roosevelt, who called his predecessor "a great patriot and a great soul." There were many stencils from the writings of Theodore Roosevelt on the walls of the frescoed auditorium, but perhaps of more significance to me than any of these was a quotation which appeared in the President's address: "A great democracy must be progressive or it will soon cease to be either great or democratic." I thought of the fifteen million Americans of my color

(276)

patiently waiting for democracy to come along and take them in.

I assisted in another display of the democratic spirit in 1940, when the Library of Congress and the Gertrude Clarke Whittall Foundation held a festival of literature, art, and music to commemorate the seventy-fifth anniversary of the proclamation of the Constitutional Amendment which abolished slavery. Dorothy Maynor opened the evening concert series and I concluded it. The general theme of the festival, the contribution of American Negroes to American culture, compelled me once again to think about the environment in which my race has had to make its way.

In white circles, people speak of the Negro Problem. The Negro Problem means to white people: What are we going to do with the Negroes? To us it means something else. It means: How can we advance ourselves in a social and political order of which we are the voiceless ten per cent? The white population worries about us because we are so numerous, although the census of 1940 shows there is not a single state in which we are not outnumbered; and we worry about ourselves for the same reason, if not to the same purpose. White people are afraid we might muster too many votes. We get discouraged because there are so many of us to feed and clothe and house and educate. Some of us even worry because we think we ought to be making a greater contribution to American culture. We have, we think, the quality; but we find ourselves hindered by dependence within and reluctance without.

Diego Rivera, the Mexican painter, has said of various efforts to show North American art to the Latin Americans that the three North American cultures which might be of interest to them were conspicuously absent from official expositions: the Indian, the Negro, and (in transplanted form) the Oriental. The Latin Americans, he said, are able to go to the European sources directly, for themselves. What they are interested in at present is art which is native to the Americas; and I think it is true that they have been somewhat ahead of us in the study and appreciation of those native source materials. I believe we possess many rich qualities in our own country, and I wish we could learn to treasure them. I can speak for our Negro culture, because I have been exposed to it, and it is my idea that we Negroes can make a beginning by rediscovering it ourselves. Then we can ask our white brothers to take notice of it.

I am glad that pride of race has lately been growing amongst us. Many of us are conscious of being descended from an ancient people which early reached a high degree of culture. I remember with what eagerness

I Renew My Vow at Angel Mo' Farm

I read in Munich all the works of Leo Frobenius, the anthropologist whose *African Genesis* has been in circulation in English amongst us for the last five years. My mother had brought me up on a combination of Negro music and Hebrew Scripture. From Frobenius I discovered that we Negroes had a mythology of our own, of greater antiquity and no less respectability.

As the African *mythos* has come to us in writing, it is compounded with Islamic and other Semitic matter, but many of its roots are purely Negro. As old as Adam (A Man) and Eve (Life, hence Mother of Life) are the First Man and the First Woman of African lore. In Hebrew and African mythology alike, Knowledge, both sensual and abstract, flows from a woman's curiosity. In the Hebrew Genesis, Adam and Eve are naked and unashamed. They do not know what their bodies are for. Then inquisitive Eve, "poor, motherless Eve," learns from the Serpent that she can easily find out why Adam is different from her. She eats an apple from the Tree of Knowledge and gives one to Adam to eat. They see their bodies and become embarrassed, and thus the story reaches a high moral plane. After a while the descendants of the first Semitic parents begin to wonder where heaven and earth came from. They decide that God made them. So the Book of Genesis also begins on a high religious plane.

Angel Mo' and Her Son, Roland Hayes

My own ancestors were earthier. The First Man and First Woman of Africa lived under the surface of the earth. They did not see each other until one day when they came up out of the ground at the same time to draw water. According to the legend, they were not at all embarrassed. They lay together for eight days. Every year the woman bore the man four sons or four daughters, until she had given birth to a hundred children. It is surprising that after such a realistic beginning, the First Man and the First Woman should have let their children go out into the world without telling them anything about the facts of life, but their reticence is a matter of record. Like the sons and daughters of Baptist parents in the Flatwoods, their offspring had to learn about those things for themselves.

A girl and a boy of that generation, according to tradition, discovered the implications of sex for themselves, and although it was admitted that they were benefactors of society, even African sensibility required the girl to become a witch and the boy a man-eating lion.

The remaining forty-nine sons and forty-nine daughters entered upon a more settled life and began to ask questions about the world around them. It was a woman who produced the classically pragmatic answers to the questions of the first Negro philosopher. The earth, she said, produced her own waters and rocks and plants: because the earth was already here. It was a sensible, female answer which satisfied my people well enough until injury sent them to God. Like the Hebrews, who began to believe in life hereafter because the terms of life here were too hard, the enslaved Africans in America learned to find comfort in the thought of one day entering a spiritual world where they would be free in Christ.

But for all our native scriptures and our simple religious faith, we Negroes remain as we began: of the soil, earthy, and I am glad of it. I should not be happy if all of our impulses were derived, like the white man's, from the brain. Our earliest tradition shows us to have been apt in agriculture, which we learned from the ant; in killing wild animals which we could not tame; and in the husbandry of gentler cattle whom the ant had taught to be respectful of mankind. We learn this lore from an abundant remainder of prehistoric art, rich in animal devices, and all of these gifts we Negroes still retain.

IV

The pride of race of which I speak has unfortunately not yet — considering our numbers — produced much contemporary Negro art in any field. Back in 1926

Angel Mo' and Her Son, Roland Hayes

Langston Hughes, whose poem, "The Negro Speaks of Rivers," Percival Parham set to music for me, told Carl Sandburg, who was writing then for the *Chicago News*, that Negroes had failed to do creative work in music, literature, and art whenever they had set themselves to copy the style of white men. The trouble has been that there have been so few American Negro models to follow, and we do not seem to be able to make the intellectual effort necessary for the creation of more. In the plastic arts, Africa and the islands of the Caribbean have produced an abundance of original forms, contemporary and archaic. When I saw Paul Guillaume's collection of African arts and crafts in Paris a few years ago, I thought to myself, "Why can we not produce such things at home?"

I suppose it is natural for me, an artist, to think that the Negro's innate usefulness to the common cultural life of our country lies in agriculture and processing, in craftsmanship and the arts, rather than in politics; and by politics I mean not specifically the holding of offices, but more generally the whole field of civil relationships. Mary White Ovington writes that the Negro is "only half a man," because his citizenship is only partial. She is profoundly right. But it is my notion that we should fight for the vote not for the sake of forming a Negro bloc, on competitive terms with farm blocs and silver

blocs and ecclesiastical blocs, but simply so that we shall
be able to procure for ourselves ampler means for the
expression of our peculiar gifts. We need to vote money
for our schools so that we can have better teachers. We
need more money for library services so that we may
be better informed. At present, the city of Jackson,
Mississippi, for example, spends exactly one cent a year,
per capita, on the maintenance of library facilities for
Negroes. We can probably get what we need only
through the exercise of franchise. Still, there are many
things which we ought to be doing with our own
money. We could operate more hospitals, endow more
scholarships for our children. We must be willing to
spend ourselves out on our own.

I realize that it is not easy for us to get hold of spare
capital. Colored people receive less money than white
people for the same services. It takes longer to save up
and get ahead. But what of that? Like the Chinese, we
are no respecters of time. Our activities are regulated
by the immutable laws of axile rotation and sidereal
revolution which govern the getting up and going to
bed of white people, but we may be thankful that,
compared to our white brothers, we submit to the operation of those laws with something less of personal in-
convenience.

Although I am not unsympathetic with pro-Negro

lobbies, I do not expect that we shall be saved by law, I cannot believe that our most urgent need is the enactment of new laws by white legislators. At the risk of being called reactionary, I want to reiterate my faith that we shall be saved by our own work and not as wards of the Government. I feel about the Negro problem the way a missionary feels about the Christian religion. In the back of every missionary's mind, there is a dream of bringing all the world to Christ, but in practice he goes out after converts one by one. In the same way, we Negroes must reach the hearts of white folks singly. Every once in a while one of us may make a convert who, like the Emperor Constantine, will draw souls after him.

Something of the sort happened to me in 1939, when I gave my services for a benefit concert in Calhoun, Georgia, for the Rosenwald School for Negroes and the local troop of white boy scouts. The Georgia journalists were holding a convention there at the time, and a good many editors came to my recital, together with a fair sprinkling of boys from the back room. An editor of the conservative *Atlanta Constitution* wrote a piece about me, in effect a history of the Negroes from the time of Sherman's March to the present. "And now in this day," he concluded, in substance, "white people sit in the same room with Negroes to hear the voice of the son of a slave, a black man who contributes to the education of black and white children alike."

I do not mean to suggest that the state of Georgia was thereupon converted. The Negro press, with whatever justification, has persisted in calling the present war a "white man's war." All but a few Negro soldiers continue to say, "We cannot defend America with a dust brush, a mop, and a white apron." And in reply to this challenge to our national safety, men in high places in my state, and elsewhere — not in Washington, thank God! — have replied, "Yes, this *is* a white man's war. So what?" Many a missionary has gone from the pulpit into the cauldron of the cannibal.

I have no doubt that some of my people will think I have understated my private vexations. Stones have been thrown through the windows of my house in Brookline; I have been refused a bed in a hotel in Tucson, a chair in a Seattle lobby, a meal in a restaurant in Duluth; and once, not so long ago, I was beaten and thrown into jail. But I see no good in reciting the details of a thousand such misadventures. A white minister of religion came to interview me for a church journal while I was dining alone in my room in the Duluth hotel. He asked me whether I had been requested to stay out of the public dining room. I admitted that I had been so ordered. The minister wanted to "take it up" with somebody.

"There is nothing you can do," I said. "That is a job for me and my own people."

In the summer of 1938 a young Canadian pupil wanted to continue his studies with me at Angel Mo' Farm. I said that if he went to Georgia with me, neither of us would come away alive. But I allowed him to overpersuade me. I let him come and live in back of a store on my place. A white farmer soon warned me that he had heard in a near-by town a threat to throw us out.

"You ought to know," he said, "that white people and niggers don't live together down here."

I pointed to a cottage back of the store.

"Do you see that house?" I asked. "A white man, a Southern white man, lives in that cottage and works on my farm. And over there is another white tenant, and yonder another. They are there of their own choice. So is my pupil here of his own choice. Why don't you run them all out?"

But I sent my pupil away. I had to. I had to obey an unwritten law over which, whatever its inconsistencies, I had no control. Ten years earlier, Oswald Garrison Villard had written a magazine article called "The Crumbling Color Line." I wanted to write him a letter:

I Renew My Vow at Angel Mo' Farm

"Ain't seen much crumblin' down this way, Mr. Villard."

Yes, there have been passages in my life when it would have been easy to turn back; and times, no doubt, when I felt impelled to turn and rend the adversary. About ten years ago I took it into my head to retire, and for two or three years I appeared infrequently in the concert halls. Today, I feel I must go on, for now more than ever the case for the Negro must be brought to the public: by the Congressman and the lawyer and the writer in their way, by me in mine. National policy today is being directed towards a more generous treatment of Negroes, in the Services and in industrial life, and it rests with each of us to persuade the country that there is value and justice in the new direction from Washington.

Now I am brought to the confession that my eye is no longer single. When I am not actually singing, with my mind on one object, I am down at Angel Mo' with my eye on another. But I think Ma would forgive me, for it is the war that divides me. I have been timbering off Horn's Mountain to make defense lumber, and I can do anything there from stump to stack. Acting upon the ineluctable principle that race is nothing where there is necessity, I hire white men and black men indiscriminately — neighboring farmers who need a little extra cash

(287)

for their farms. I go out into the woods myself and mark the trees to be felled, for I do not want to strip the Mountain. Then the stumpers go out and saw them down and cut them up. We log with a tractor which snakes the timbers down from mountainside to mill. A sawyer feeds the logs to a rotary saw and off-bearers carry the green lumber away and stack it. Some of the lumber goes straight to the market in Chattanooga, for war projects, and what is not wanted there finds its way, after it dries out, into new tenant cottages on my expanding farm.

Pretty soon I am going to have a gristmill. Corn cannot be ground within ten miles of my place, and many of my neighbors have no conveyance. After the war I shall build a sorghum mill as well, for already I am putting some of my acres into sorghum cane. When the cane is ripe, you strip down the leaves and feed the bare stalks into the mill. The juice runs out into a long copper pan in which it simmers into syrup over graded fires, to become the prime sweetener in my country. Give me a dish of black-eyed peas boiled with sidemeat, a plate of cornbread, and a pitcher of sorghum, and I will fell a tree or sing a concert against any man twenty years younger.

Just now, what with all the importunity of war, we have to use machines at Angel Mo' to get our work done quickly. But I am wondering whether, after the war, it would not be a good thing to rid the farm of tractors and give work to more men with mules. We can treat the earth more tenderly when we are closer to it, and we can keep the taste of metal out of our mouths and the smell of gasoline out of our valley. And besides, when all is said and done, we are more at home with our feet in the furrow. We Negroes were not meant to congregate in cities. Whenever the machine has brought us together so that we have had to live in large numbers in city tenements, we have gone against nature. I do not mean that we are inept with machines. On the contrary, many of us love gadgets and have a knack with them. But we are not at home in crowded industrial places.

Although some of us have got into trouble and had to pay with the grass rope and the hickory tree, we are naturally a gentle and imaginative people, when you come to know us. Tragedy may stalk our houses, but Comedy lives handily around the corner. We could not be sane if we had not made his acquaintance. Violence sometimes emerges from our teeming quarters and ranges our streets, peering with fierce confusion impartially at life and death; but give him elbowroom and he will share the sidewalk with Politeness, his neighbor. As my Angel Mother used to say, some of us are Christian folks and some are vagabonds, but all of us are people.

COM